The Sophisticated Sock

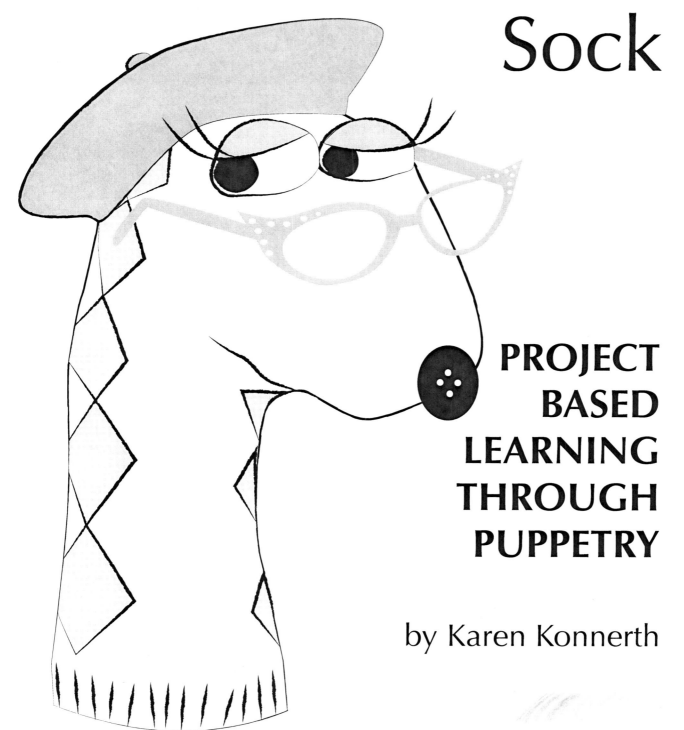

**PROJECT
BASED
LEARNING
THROUGH
PUPPETRY**

by Karen Konnerth

ACKNOWLEDGEMENTS

I wish to thank the children of New Orleans, who enthusiastically showed me the value of introducing my art form into their classrooms and I wish to thank the teachers who envisioned and supported puppetry as an integral part of their curriculum.

Special thanks to Mrs. Norma Bemiss of St. Mary's Academy Elementary School in her uniquely creative efforts to make this my lab school, allowing us to share our own vision of a just world with these wonderfully creative children.

Thanks to Mr. E. Frank Bluestein and the Tennessee Arts Academy for inviting me to present the teacher workshop series which became this book.

Special thanks to Linda Cook, Registered Drama Therapist/Board Certified Trainer and past-president North American Drama Therapy Association, and to Judith O'Hare, Puppeteers of America Education Consultant, for editing work and to Jean Kuecher of Jean Kuecher's Marionette Playhouse for puppetry in education support and encouragement.

DEDICATION

To my parents who led me to have no doubt in my own creativity

CONTACT: www.karenkonnerth.com

ISBN 978-0-9816510-1-9

Published in the United States of America by PaperSunPress

All drawings and photographs by author, except back cover photo by Vic Shepherd

TABLE OF CONTENTS

Introduction to Puppetry Themes

Language Arts Themes

TABLE OF CONTENTS

Social Studies and History Themes

Science Themes

Art Themes

Conflict Resolution Theme

FOREWORD

Karen Konnerth's world-traveling adventures in puppetry would fill a book. I'm so glad she has focused some of that experience on this treasure, <u>The Sophisticated Sock,</u> showing how to gain a world of educational value through simple-to-make puppets.

Karen is an expert guide to puppetry in the classroom, from lesson planning with curriculum focused expected learning outcomes, to clear teaching, reflection, and assessment of project-based learning. And she provides wonderful ideas on how to make tradition-rooted puppets out of everyday materials.

She is an illustrator and writer as well as puppeteer, and the various storytelling templates develop writing skills to help all ages hold an audience. Teachers especially will appreciate Karen's illustrated project choices for different skill and age levels. And while it would be possible to teach directly from Karen's page-by-page advice, I believe the book's greater use will be to give teachers the confidence to create their own puppetry lessons in open-ended activities.

The Sophisticated Sock is an invaluable teaching tool for inspiration in the discovery of puppetry, an old and yet ever-new art form that, as Karen shows, includes every other form of art. Enjoy!

— Jan Wolfe

President, Puppeteers of America

If you are looking at this book…

- as a teacher overwhelmed with assessment pressure, you are wondering how you could ever find time for arts projects.

- as a teaching artist with limited time to see each class, you are wondering how you could have significant impact to support core standards learning.

- as a youth leader outside of a school, you are wondering how you could implement projects to develop life skills such as cooperation and creative thinking.

This book is designed specifically for all of you in offering time-efficient, step-by-step projects to produce memorable, in-depth, core standards-based, collaborative learning. The magically engaging art form of puppetry is the Pied Piper requiring students to grasp, use, and therefore, remember the curriculum core of each lesson in order to bring the art form to life. STEAM (Science, Technology, Engineering, Art, Math) learning takes place as students manipulate and experiment with materials for a specific purpose and every project necessitates higher order thinking skills including analysis, evaluation, creation, logical reasoning, judgment, critical thinking, and problem solving.

This section contains information about:

INTRODUCTION

Why This Book Was Written

When I added teaching artist to my years of performing puppeteer experience, I found an immediate bridge between the curriculum content I was asked to tackle and the ancient and infinitely adaptable art form of puppetry. I found students willing and enthusiastic to read, write, research, cooperate, self organize, and, most important, think deeply, in order to present learning through puppetry. And because puppetry is a theatrical art form, although there are layers of learning in the story formation and puppet building experience, there is always the performance, no matter how informal, as the motivating end goal that can be assessed.

Working as visiting artist in a wide variety of schools, with diverse ages and populations, I was asked by teachers to connect to many different themes and curriculum areas. It is through these experiences that this book was written. These active learning frameworks have all been refined, revised, and adapted in multiple classroom projects over many years in collaboration and consultation with many educators. Each project, as well as puppet building technique, considers the school reality of time as well as budget in providing a realistic, in-depth, assessable learning experience.

How To Use This Book

The book is organized into three sections:
II. Activities and Projects
Activities One through Three are hands-on introductions to how a puppet
   communicates, connecting to emotional, visual, and aural literacy.
Projects Four through Fifteen are core standards based and include reproducible
   worksheets, assessment, and performance criteria, as well as suggestions for puppet
   technique choice. They are organized by themes under Language Arts, Social Studies
   and History, Science, Art, and Conflict Resolution.
III. Puppet Making Techniques
The puppet technique section features detailed diagrams and explanations for tradition-
   based, quick, simple puppets using easily available, recycled or inexpensive materials.
IV. Supplemental Materials and Resources
Find here instructions and organizational tools referred to in the projects as well as
   some favorite reference books.

To Begin:

Consider:
   - what core content area you would like to augment with puppetry
   - your students' age
   - number of students in class
   - time available
   - space available
   - budget and available materials

Examine: the Activities and Projects section to find a connection you would like to use, or adapt, to your curriculum.

Projects:
- are clustered for grades K – 2 and 3 – 5
- vary from single session experiences, to sequential series

All projects include:
- core standards based center
- clear goals and objectives
- puppet construction
- culminating performance or event
- reflection
- assessment
- cooperative learning

Select: a puppet building technique, either from suggestions in the project description, or choose another from the Puppet Making Techniques section.
Make sure that the technique selected leaves time for the culminating presentation or performance - to allow an authenic experience in puppet theater!

Prepare materials as directed in the project and duplicate necessary worksheets (which immediately follow the lesson).

Introduce the project to the students, using brief included scripts as desired.

You CAN Do This: Sample Project Ideas

First graders use file folders, fabric scraps, thin rods, and small balls to bring to life an interdependant community of table top puppets who develop business relationships, trade goods and services, write their own laws, and explain their role in the community to visitors in a school wide event.

Third graders analyze poetry and prepare it for a theatrical performance using miscellaneous materials to create concrete and abstract rod puppets inspired by the text for expressive movement with narrations.

Kindergartners use simple hand puppets to experience story sequence through performance of individual scenes from a familiar tale, presented to a peer audience.

Fifth graders use large scale miming puppets made of recycled materials to demonstrate choices in the resolution of realistic conflicts for presentation at a school behavior awards event.

Each fourth grade class uses shadow puppets to share myths and folktales of a different culture, to share and explain the cultural roots and traditions in a Celebration of Culture event.

Second graders work with a partner to decorate a cardboard box toy theater representing a natural environment, then use paper puppets to show the effect of man made changes on the animals living there for a dynamic Science Fair project.

What is a Puppet?

A puppet is any object brought to life by a person to communicate an idea or story to an audience. A puppet must be used as a vehicle to transport ideas from one imagination to another, not as a static object or sculpture, but as a being that lives, breathes, and feels, in the imagination of a living, breathing, feeling viewer. Whether complex and beautiful, or elementary and crude, when an object is brought to life as a communicator, it is a puppet. A puppet communicates through:

• movement
• visual appearance
• voice or sound
• story (or connected sequential events)

What is Puppet Theater?

Puppet theater is an ancient form of theater using manipulated objects to communicate with audiences of adults and/or children. Puppetry has allowed people to create expressive worlds for over 2,000 years globally. Traditions in puppetry vary tremendously in manner of moving the puppet, in materials used, in purpose of the performance, in type of stories or ideas shared, in size of the performing troupe, and many other aspects.

I have been asked more than once "Isn't puppetry a dying art form?" Although far less commonly seen today than the ubiquitous screen, the attraction to live puppet theater remains strong simply because it is live. Video recorded puppetry becomes film – a totally different medium. Live puppet theater is two-way communication in which the puppeteer is acutely aware of the audience response, and the audience is totally willing to suspend all disbelief to enter into the reality of an alternate world. The audience becomes emotionally involved and experiences empathy through the power of the story. Of course a movie may have a similar effect, however, the accessibility of the three dimensional puppets in the audience's own three-dimensional world creates an irresistible desire to believe in the impossible – the attraction that puppet theater has always had.

Why Puppets in School Classrooms?

• **Puppets are fun.**

Puppets immediately engage imagination and spark creative thinking – a higher order thinking skill.

• **Writing for performance makes core content memorable.**

Puppetry integrated across the curriculum necessitates use of the higher order thinking skill of analyzation of core content in order to communicate learning in performance.

• **Performance experiences reveal standards of excellence.**

Another higher order thinking skill, evaluation, sharpens as students observe degrees of effective performance elements first hand.

• **Puppetry teamwork necessitates development of basic life skills.**

In contemporary society, workers at all levels are required to be creative thinkers, problem solvers, able to work well with others, and able to work independently. They must also be self-motivated and pro-active – all skills developed in collaborative puppetry work.

• **Puppetry accommodates learners in all styles.**

The diversity of communication styles that comes together in the aspects of visual and tactile form, sound, story, and movement which is puppetry, encourages verbal, visual, aural, and kinesthetic learners.
• **Puppetry projects can provide an assessable culmination.**
When students analyze core content in order to build a collaborative, theatrical work to communicate learning, the performance piece becomes an assessable finale.

A Note about Classroom Management
From my personal experience in many classrooms, the students' enthusiasm at the opportunity to work with puppetry is a powerful leverage tool. I emphasize the crucial importance of self-discipline and delineate specific expectations, as outlined in the project checklists. I have found that disruptive or irresponsible behavior improves markedly if the individual must sit out an experience, or temporarily lose access to their puppet.
I emphasize that puppets DO NOT fight – which is the peculiar, but very common instinctual first reaction to a puppet. I highly recommend Activity One as an introduction, as this gives purpose to puppet movement.

This point also relates to the tendency in story writing for students, especially boys, to be stuck on themes "needing" weapons or violence for the characters to solve the problem. My strategy is to tell students that, yes, this is what you see in many movies and games, but you must be more creative than these writers and find violence and weapon-free solutions. Some students have no idea what to do within my framework, but generally (sometimes with prompting) figure out alternate solutions.

I consider the requirement to solve story problems with-out violence as a step in development of a life skill.

A NOTE ABOUT CREATIVITY

We are all born creative people, and live our lives constantly making creative decisions - whether on how to cook a dinner from the leftovers in the refrigerator, how to keep the attention of a class of 30 distinct individuals, or how we want to communicate an idea in a poem, a drawing, a song, or a puppet.
It is essential for the people who will be solving the problems of the future to have confidence in their creative thinking.
Therefore, to expect the most from a class, it is crucial to realize and to model pride in one's own creative ability.
Additionally, it is crucial to be open and accepting of creative work by all students. There is more than one way to solve just about any problem and art experiences are an excellent way to learn this.
Therefore all of these activities must be conducted with an underlying understanding that each person will give their best effort, and that this deserves attention and respect.

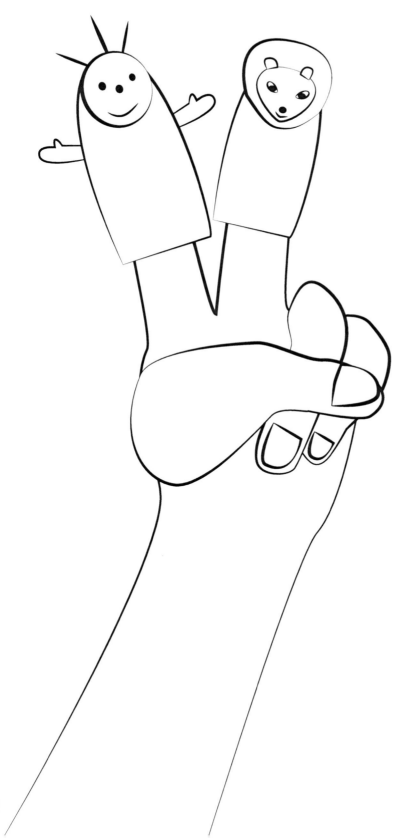

This section is the essence of the book.

These activities and projects are the glue that binds core standards content to memorable, engaged learning.

To begin, you will find an index of the projects including the driving question and a brief overview. The index listings include a time estimate, which is variable depending on the puppet technique selected, the size and age of the class. This index also shows page numbers for easy access to the supplemental pages to duplicate for the specific project. All worksheets or resource pages essential to that project follow the full description. There are a few additional resources that are used in several projects which you will be directed to in the Supplements and Resources final section of the book.

The core content strands along with goals and objectives are found within the full description of each activity or project plan along with a recommended puppet construction plan from Section III Puppet Making Techniques.

Activities One through Three introduce the main expressive elements of puppetry as connected to emotional, visual, and auditory literacy. They are a little bit silly, very engaging, and quickly effective in making a point, with slightly different versions for K - 1 and for 2 - 5.
Activity One involves thoughtful observation of human gesture, or body language, in the expression of emotions and transfers that awareness to give life to a formless puppet.
If your time is limited, I highly recommend at least a quick experience with Activity One so that children understand the purpose of a puppet. (Skipping the mask section is an option - going directly from full body to hand gesture).

Projects Three through Fifteen are built around core content themes you may use in various Language Arts, Social Studies and History, Science, Art, or Conflict Resolution projects.

All Activities and Projects include optional scripted introductions you may use if you like.

So, please look over the themes, core contents, and goals and objectives until something captures your imagination!

ACTIVITIES AND PROJECTS

Introduction to Puppetry Themes

Language Arts Themes

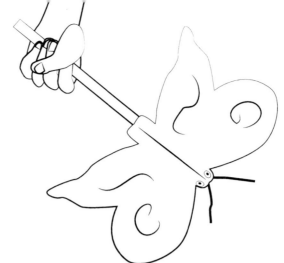

Art Themes

Conflict Resolution Theme

ACTIVITY ONE: FROM SKIP TO STOMP
Driving Question: How do we use our bodies to communicate emotions?

Grades: K - 1, 2 - 5

Overview
Students participate in creative dramatics games to study how we use our bodies unconsciously to express emotions, culminating in using a puppet to express emotions.

Grades Kindergarten through First work with simple emotion diagrams to act out with their whole bodies, then use a very simple puppet to express the same emotions.

Grades Two through Five work with one of two grade appropriate emotion vocabulary lists to mime emotions for the class to guess – first using the whole body, then eliminating facial expressions with a neutral mask, then translated to improvisations with a simple puppet.

Core Standards: Language Arts:
Reading: Integration of Knowledge and Ideas
Speaking and Listening: Comprehension and Collaboration; Presentation of Knowledge and Ideas
Foundation Skill:
Emotional Literacy: The ability to identify, understand, and respond to emotions in oneself and others in a healthy manner

---

Expected Learning Outcomes:
Students will be able to demonstrate body posture and action to show emotions.
Students will be able to analyze and articulate body posture details of others as it communicates emotions.
Students will be able to dramatize suggested scenes with the movement of a puppet.

VOCABULARY:

Emotion:
a strong feeling, often in reaction to an event

Body Language:
movements or positions of a person's body that expresses thoughts or feelings

Mask:
a cover for the face used to hide the identity of a person

Puppet:
an object operated by a person to express ideas, emotions, or story to another

Improvise:
to create a performance in the moment, without script

GRADES K – 1
TIME: 30 - 45 minutes

ORGANIZE AND PREPARE
1. **SELECT** puppet making technique and gather materials.
QUICKEST: Sock Full Body design (p.143) **BUT without** any decorations – just the tiny holes cut in the sides. The students could complete these for another project later on.
Other options would be plain socks, gloves, or mittens.
LONGER: undecorated, sewn fabric hand puppets (pattern p.141)
2. **PRINT:** Body Language Clues Level 1 (p.22), one per student

---

INTRODUCE PART 1
Can you tell, just by looking at someone, if they are happy? sad? angry? proud? When you do that, you are reading body language. Without even thinking about it, we use our bodies to communicate our emotions.

DISTRIBUTE Body Language Clues Level 1 Sheets

On the activity sheet, can you figure out how the character is feeling in each drawing? Now, two people at a time will demonstrate for us. We will give them an emotion word and they will show us with their bodies how it looks to feel that way. If they need help, we can make suggestions. For example, a sad person might have their head down. An angry person might stomp their feet. A shy person might not want to look at the audience. Let's try this! Can you think of any other emotion words to act out?

SHARE
All students have turn both acting, and guessing.

INTRODUCE PART 2
I am putting something in front of you. Do not touch it yet.
(PLACE sock, glove, or mitten in front of each student.)
When you put these on your hands, we will pretend that your hands turn into new creatures. They will be able to express emotions through movement, as you just did. Carefully put them on your hands.

SHARE
All students experience guided activity.
(Speak slowly, giving time for students' creatures to express each segment.)
They are still sleeping. When they wake up, at first they are shy. Show this by their movement. Are they hiding their faces? their whole bodies? Now they are angry. They do not touch each other. (etc. through various emotions, finally back to sleep).

REFLECT
How did you use different parts of your body to show happiness, sadness, anger? How did you show those feelings with the puppets?

ASSESS
Teacher: Performance based

GRADES 2 – 5
TIME: one to three 45 minute class sessions.
Larger classes and younger children may need multiple sessions to complete all three activities, to allow each child time to participate. Younger children may also need more time to make the masks.

ORGANIZE AND PREPARE
1. Gather materials for:
* Masks (p.148)
* Puppets:
QUICKEST: Sock Full Body design (p.143) WITHOUT ANY DECORATION – just the tiny holes cut in sides. The students could complete these for another project later on.
Other options would be plain socks, gloves, or mittens.
LONGER: undecorated, sewn fabric hand puppets (pattern p.141), one/student
2. **PRINT:**
• one copy Body Language Clues Level 2 OR 3 (as appropriate) (p.23 or 24)
• Emotions and Movement Self Evaluation, one/student (p.25)

INTRODUCE PART 1
Can you tell, just by looking at someone, if they are happy? sad? angry? proud? When you do that, you are reading body language. Without even thinking about it, we use our bodies to communicate our emotions. We will play a game today to study how we do that. Then we will use what we learned to show emotions through a simple puppet.
This is a silent game. You are each going to work with a partner. You and your partner will have a turn to hear or read a secret word – an emotion or feeling. Then, together, you will walk across the room in front of the class SILENTLY, using only your face and body movements, to act out that word. You need to try to make it as easy as possible for the class to guess the word.
The class will watch and guess what your word is. When anyone thinks they have guessed the word, they will not shout out, but raise their hand to be called on. Please treat your classmates with respect.

SHARE
1. Select two students to come to the front of the room. (One person at a time is fine, but most are more comfortable working with a partner. If time is short, three is fine, too.)
2. Holding list out of sight of class, point to one adjective from the list (whisper to non-readers). It may help to ask that they imagine a time when they felt this way. Emphasize that the point of the game is to make it as easy as possible for the class to guess - not to trick them.
3. Students walk across the front of the room using their body and face (no sound) to express the assigned word.
4. Call on students to guess the feeling expressed. When the correct word has been guessed, ask for a specific description - Shoulders back? chin up? moving with or without energy? smiling? (Notice that surprised and scared are best shown as a reaction TO something.)

20

REFLECT

Can you describe something you noticed about body language for showing a specific emotion?

CREATE

Each student makes a paper plate mask. (p.148) DO NOT decorate the mask. These are "Neutral Masks", simply to hide the face. *I recommend preventing access to markers or any drawing materials.*

INTRODUCE PART 2

You have been using your whole body to express feelings, but now you will have less to work with. You will still express feelings, but without the use of one part - the face. How do you think this will change the game? Why?

SHARE

Play the same game again, now with participants wearing masks to hide facial expressions.

REFLECT

Did you do anything differently, knowing that the audience could not see your face?

INTRODUCE PART 3 (AND SHARE)

I am putting something in front of you. Do not touch it yet.
(PLACE sock, glove, or mitten in front of each student.)
(Speak slowly, giving time for students' creatures to express each segment.)
Now, the only part of you that can express feelings is one hand. This hand is about to become the skeleton and muscles of a brand new creature. On the table in front of you is the skin of this creature. Put the skin on. The creatures are all asleep. They are breathing. (All students should now have the glove on their hand, with hand quietly on the table in front of them). *These creatures cannot make any sounds, but they can see, hear, touch, smell, taste, and feel. They may not touch each other. They begin to wake up.* (show in movement) *They FEEL the smooth tabletop.* (react) *They SEE the light.* (react) *They are sad to be all alone* (react). *They are afraid to see other creatures* (react). *They are shy. Then they are angry. They decide the other creatures seem friendly. They are happy.* (all shown in movement). *They go back to sleep. Now take off the skins and you are once more able to use your whole body to express emotions.*

REFLECT

You just brought to life a very simple puppet. How would you use what you just experienced if you were telling a story with puppets?

ASSESS

Teacher: Performance based
Students Grades 2 - 5: Self Evaluation: Emotions and Movement (p.25)

EVERY DAY BODY LANGUAGE
Find Scared, Mad, Shy, Sad, Tired, Happy.

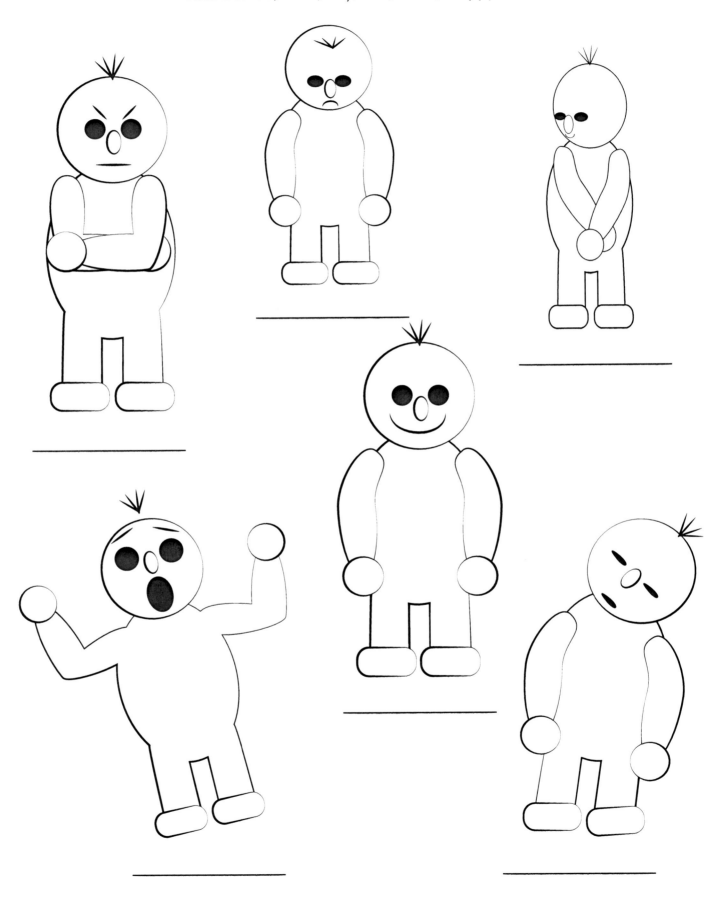

BODY LANGUAGE CUES LEVEL 2

HAPPY	HOT
SAD	SURPRISED
SCARED	BORED
PROUD	NERVOUS
SHY	BOSSY
ANGRY	WEAK
COLD	TIRED
SLEEPY	STRONG

JOYOUS	BORED
DESPONDENT	ANXIOUS
TERRIFIED	DOMINEERING
PROUD	PUNY
BASHFUL	FATIGUED
IRATE	BRAWNY
FROSTY	FRUSTRATED
DROWSY	SERENE
SWELTERING	INDUSTRIOUS
ASTOUNDED	IDLE

Name _____ Date _____

How Did I Do?
EMOTIONS AND MOVEMENT

Circle the number of stars that you think best describe your work for each question.

AS A THINKER

1. I watched my classmates carefully to figure out what emotion they were expressing.

    *   ***   *****

2. I thought about how I use my own body to express emotions to others.

    *   ***   *****

AS A PERFORMER

3. I used movement thoughtfully to express emotions using my own body.

    *   ***   *****

4. I used movement thoughtfully to express emotions with my puppet.

    *   ***   *****

AS AN AUDIENCE MEMBER

5. I identified emotions shown by my classmates' body movements.

    *   ***   *****

6. I used words to describe specific things they were doing to help guess their word.

    *   ***   *****

7. I raised my hand when I had a response.

    *   ***   *****

8. I was polite and thoughtful in my comments.

    *   ***   *****

_____

9. My thoughts on the experience (use back of paper if needed):

ACTIVITY TWO: FROM SMOOTH TO POINTY
Driving Question: How can shape and color build an expressive character?

Grades: K - 2, 3 - 5

Overview
Students use geometric shapes to create an abstract puppet character then bring it to life in an improvised scene.

Grades Kindergarten through First assemble pre-cut geometric shapes to form an imaginary animal to introduce to the class.

Grades Two through Five experience the expressive power of shape, and possibly color, in building a character to represent one of a contrasting pair of antonyms to dramatize with a partner.

GRADES K – 2
TIME: one 45 minute class session

ORGANIZE AND PREPARE

VOCABULARY:
Geometric Shapes:
Square
Circle
Triangle
Oval
Rectangle, etc.
Shape Adjectives:
Pointy
Jagged
Smooth
Straight
Rounded
Abstract: representing an idea or mood, rather than concrete object
Expressive: able to show emotion or mood
Profile: side view of a face

1. **SELECT** a puppet technique and gather materials.
QUICKEST: Shadow Puppets: Assembled Shapes (p.156)
LONGER: Rod Puppets: Assembled Shapes (p.153)
2. **SELECT** a focus illustrated book featuring lots of animals. *A favorite of mine is **If I Ran the Zoo**, by Dr. Seuss – for the imagination stretching animals.*

INTRODUCE

For thousands of years, people have told stories with puppets made of whatever materials they had available including clay, leather, wood, cloth, even recycled plastic. Today we will use paper scraps. You will each put together these paper shapes to make an imaginary animal of your choice. You will name your animal, and know where it lives and what it eats. First, you may get some ideas from this book.

CORE STANDARDS: LANGUAGE ARTS:
Reading: Integration of Knowledge and Ideas; Speaking and Listening: Comprehension and Collaboration; Presentation of Knowledge and Ideas
MATH: Make sense of problems and persevere in solving them.
Reason abstractly and quantitatively.
FOUNDATION SKILL: Visual Literacy: The ability to understand, create, and use visual images

Expected Learning Outcomes:
Students will be able to demonstrate body posture and action to show emotions.
Students will be able to analyze and articulate body posture details of others as it communicates emotions.
Students will be able to dramatize suggested scenes with the movement of a puppet.

FOCUS

Read selected book, discussing animals' appearance (feet, horns, tails, etc.) as well as where they find what they need to survive.

CREATE

Make puppets of pre-cut geometric shapes. NOTE: These should be PROFILE, or SIDE view (showing only one eye, with nose protruding) so that puppet characters may clearly face each other for interaction. Decorate BOTH sides of construction paper shapes.

SHARE

In a formal or informal puppet stage area, interview each new animal, allowing it to describe its favorite food, where it lives, etc.

REFLECT

What shapes did you notice used as parts of the puppets? Why did you choose the shapes you did to make your animal?

ASSESS

Teacher: Performance based

GRADES 3 – 5

TIME: one 45 minute class session

ORGANIZE AND PREPARE

1. Select a puppet technique and gather materials.
QUICKEST: Shadow Puppets: Constructed Shapes (p.156)
LONGER: Rod Puppets: Constructed Shapes (p.153)
PRINT:
• one copy Antonyms List (p.30) and CUT into strips of antonym pairs.
• Self Evaluation - Shapes (p.31), one/student

INTRODUCE

For thousands of years, people have told stories with puppets made of whatever materials they had available including clay, leather, wood, cloth, even recycled plastic. Today you will use paper scraps to make an expressive puppet to use in a short scene. You will each work with a partner. You and your partner will receive a pair of words that are antonyms, or opposites. Using paper shapes, you will glue them together to create a PROFILE, or side view, of your puppet face to represent your word. You will decorate BOTH sides of your puppet. Discuss with your partner: should you each use different colors? different shapes? Do pointy or rounded shapes better illustrate each word? Use your imagination! You should be able to explain why you chose the shapes and colors you did. And keep your words a secret so the class may guess your words later!

FOCUS

Distribute antonym pairs. Allow a few minutes for discussion.

CREATE

Distribute materials. Each student pair works to create a contrasting pair of puppets.

REHEARSE

Partners develop a short scene, with or without words, to further dramatize their characters through action.

SHARE

Each pair presents their scene for the class, asking class to guess their word pair.

REFLECT

What can a puppet express through visual appearance?
Why did you choose the shapes you did to make your character?
How did you use movement and sounds or words to further express your character?

ASSESS

Teacher: Performance based
Students Grades 2 - 5: Self Evaluation - Shapes (p.31)

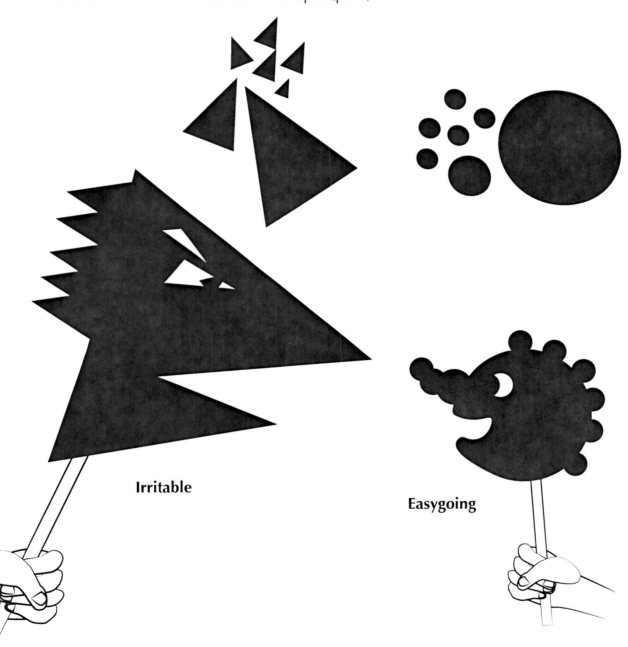

Irritable

Easygoing

angry	calm	laugh	cry
awake	asleep	nice	mean
beautiful	ugly	old	young
boring	interesting	polite	rude
brave	timid	quiet	noisy
bright	dim	rich	poor
bumpy	smooth	round	pointy
calm	nervous	scary	friendly
cruel	kind	serious	silly
enemy	friend	shy	bold
fast	slow	sick	healthy
happy	sad	sour	sweet
hard	soft	straight	curly
hate	love	tall	short
heavy	light	thin	fat
hero	coward	weak	strong
high	low	wet	dry
hot	cold	wide	narrow
large	small	wise	foolish

Name _____ Date _____

How Did I Do?
SHAPES: SIMPLE TO COMPLEX

Circle the number of stars that you think best describe your work for each question.

AS AN ART MAKER

1. I experimented with several shape combinations before deciding on a final character shape.

       *   ***   *****

2. I used my own ideas to create my character shape.

       *   ***   *****

3. I always showed respect for other students' work.

       *   ***   *****

AS A PERFORMER

4. I cooperated with other students to help bring a scene to life.

       *   ***   *****

5. I held my puppet so that the audience could see it (or it's shadow, if shadow puppet).

       *   ***   *****

AS AN AUDIENCE MEMBER

6. I watched performances quietly and thoughtfully.

       *   ***   *****

7. I raised my hand if I had a comment after each show.

       *   ***   *****

8. I was polite and thoughtful in my comments.

       *   ***   *****

9. My thoughts on the experience (use back of paper if needed):

ACTIVITY THREE: FROM SQUEAK TO ROAR
Driving Question: How much information can be communicated by the voice?

Grades: K - 1, 2 - 5

Overview
Students experience creative dramatics games using voice as an expressive tool.

Grades Kindergarten through First play the game "Whose Voice?" as they disguise their voice for classmates to try to identify the speaker.

Grades Two through Five play "Whose Voice?", followed by "Spudville", in which very simple puppets must communicate through very expressive use of only one word.

GAME ONE: WHOSE VOICE?
Time: one 30-45 minute class depending on size of class

ORGANIZE AND PREPARE

CORE STANDARDS: LANGUAGE ARTS:
Reading: Craft and Structure
Speaking and Listening: Comprehension and Collaboration; Presentation of Knowledge and Ideas
FOUNDATION SKILL: Aural Literacy: The development of critical listening skills and the analysis of sounds and their impact on our emotions and our actions.

EXPECTED LEARNING OUTCOMES:
Students will be able to distinguish differences in voices through refined listening skills.
Students will be able to create improvisational work in cooperation with others.
Students will be able to dramatize a non-verbal story using puppet movement and sound

VOCABULARY:

Unique: like no other

Accent: the way people in a particular region or country pronounce words

Imaginary: something that cannot be seen because it is in the imagination only

Prop: an object used on a theater stage or in a movie

Point of view: the voice and outlook of a particular character

1. **PRINT**
• one copy Whose Voice sheet (p.36), **cut** into three sections as marked (or use other short phrase as desired)
• The Expressive Voice Self Evaluation sheet (p.37) one/student
2. **ARRANGE** three chairs behind a simple blind (screen, bookshelf, or around a corner), so that seated participants cannot be seen by audience

INTRODUCE
People's voices sound different depending on if they are a man or a woman, a child or an adult. Voices also have different sounds unique to each individual. People may also speak with an accent because of how the people spoke where they grew up. And, our voice also communicates emotion – to sound excited, sad, scared, etc.
When you use a puppet, you may choose what kind of voice it will have. Maybe a bear would have a low voice, and a mouse a squeaky voice, or maybe it would be funny if the bear had the squeaky voice. The voice helps show the point of view of the character: who they are and what you might expect them to think or do.

We will play a game today for you to experiment to see what you can do with your voice. Three players will hide together and each take turns speaking the same words, doing their best to change their voices so the listening audience cannot tell who is speaking. The audience must remain silent. After each player has spoken, we will ask the audience for opinions on who was Player # 1, # 2, and # 3. We will then reveal the three players and see who had the best voice disguise.

SHARE

1. Three students at a time sit hidden from audience.

2. Each player says the same words, either reading from the Whose Voice sheet, or simply given any simple phrase they can remember.

3. Each player is to try to change their voice so the audience cannot recognize it as the player says the phrase.

4. After all three players have said the phrase, the audience, by raising of hands, not shouting out, is asked to identify Player # 1, # 2, and # 3 by name.

5. When the (often varying) opinions have been stated, the players reveal themselves one at a time to show the audience whether or not the guesses were correct.
NOTE: When players reveal themselves, they MUST be honest about which number player they were.

6. Repeat, until everyone has had a turn.

REFLECT

What did you do to change your voice?
What did you do to help yourself guess the voices?

GAME TWO: SPUDVILLE
Time: one 45 minute class depending on size of class

ORGANIZE AND PREPARE

1. Use neutral puppets from ACTIVITY ONE (undecorated socks, gloves or mittens, OR sewn hand puppets from pattern), one/student
2. Hand Puppet stage set up (p.146)
OPTIONAL: a few simple props found in classroom (ONE prop per GROUP). When using props, decide in advance and explain whether objects must be used only as what they are, for example a pencil is a pencil, OR if objects may be used to represent one other thing, for example, a pencil may be a cane, a tree, a baton, a trumpet – as long as the performers explain in advance what it is, and remain with this choice throughout their skit.

INTRODUCE

In this game, you will experience how your voice can express emotion. The creatures who are about to come alive are from another planet. They are very similar to us, except for one thing. Our dictionary has many words in it to express whatever we want to say. But in Spudville, they have only one word in their dictionary, so whatever they want to say can be expressed only by this one word. The word is "Potato." They can show any emotion simply by the way they say "Potato."

You are now going to work with a (one or two) partner to create a one minute scene of some characters in Spudville solving a simple problem. The scene must involve at least two emotions that the audience must clearly understand.

OPTIONAL: *You may use one **(only one)** prop* per skit as a central focus around which to build the story.*
* Props may be any small object, either collected for this purpose, or found around the classroom, to help provide a central focus to the story.

FOCUS

Students receive socks, gloves, or mittens, one per student.
Students select or are given their prop, if used.
Allow five – ten minutes for story development.

REHEARSE

Allow five-ten minutes for informal practice.

SHARE

Arrange informal audience seating and performance space.

Maintain strict audience behavior for each group to perform.

After each presentation, ask for audience reaction based on:

• What were the characters doing?

• What emotions did they show?

REFLECT

How did using only one word affect the story you could tell? As you watched performances, how could you understand characters' emotions and actions? Give specific examples.

ASSESS

Teacher: Performance based

Students Grades 2 - 5: Self Evaluation: The Expressive Voice (p.37)

WHOSE VOICE?

- -

PLAYER # 1

Sweet or scary?
Wolf or lamb?
Bet you can't guess
Who I am.

- -

PLAYER # 2

Sweet or scary?
Wolf or lamb?
Bet you can't guess
Who I am.

- -

PLAYER # 3

Sweet or scary?
Wolf or lamb?
Bet you can't guess
Who I am.

Name _____ Date _____

How Did I Do?
THE EXPRESSIVE VOICE

Circle the number of stars that you think best describe your work for each question.

AS A THINKER:

1. I listened to my classmates carefully to figure out who was speaking.

      *   ***   *****

2. I worked with my team to create a story showing at least two emotions in Spudville.

      *   ***   *****

AS A PERFORMER:

3. While playing the game, I really tried to change my voice.

      *   ***   *****

4. I used both voice and movement to help tell the story my partner(s) and I agreed on.

      *   ***   *****

AS AN AUDIENCE MEMBER:

5. I waited until I heard all three players' voices before I made a decision.

      *   ***   *****

6. I watched each performance carefully to understand the story.

      *   ***   *****

7. I was polite and thoughtful in my performance reaction comments.

      *   ***   *****

8. I raised my hand when I had a response.

      *   ***   *****

_____

9. My thoughts on the experience (use back of paper if needed):

PROJECT FOUR: FROM PAGE TO PUPPETS
Driving Question: How can we use puppets to share the events of a story?

Grades: K - 2, 3 - 5

Overview
Students learn or write a story then build puppets for a collaborative performance.
Time: Two 45 minute classes

Grades Kindergarten through Second create storyboards of a familiar tale, then make puppets to collaborate in a presentation of the story in sequetial scenes.

Grades Three through Five collaborate in specific roles to write a simple story, make puppets, and perform their work.

GRADES K - 2

ORGANIZE AND PREPARE

CORE STANDARDS: LANGUAGE ARTS
Reading: Key Ideas and Details; Craft and Structure; Integration of Knowledge and Ideas
Writing: Text Types and Purposes; Production of Writing
Speaking and Listening: Comprehension and Collaboration; Presentation of Knowledge and Ideas

EXPECTED LEARNING OUTCOMES:
Students will be able to arrange the events of a story in correct sequence.
Students will be able to determine importance in their choice of focus story elements.
Students will be able to perform collaboratively to present an assigned scene.
(Grades 3 - 5) **Students will be able to** perform a simple story demonstrating clear story structure.

VOCABULARY:

Character: who the story is about
Conflict: in a story, a problem a character must solve in order to reach their goal
Setting: where the story takes place
Critique: thoughtful comments on the work of someone else
Puppet: an object moved in performance to communicate a story or an idea to an audience
Puppeteer: a person controlling the movements of a puppet
Sequence: the order in which connected events happen
Storyboard: a series of drawings that show the sequence of events in a story.

1. **SELECT** a simple folktale, fable, or picture book with two essential characters to read aloud to the class.
Aesop's Fables are ideal because most have two characters as well as universal themes: The Hare and the Tortoise, The Lion and the Mouse, The City Mouse and the Country Mouse, The Fox and the Crow, etc.

2. **SELECT** a puppet technique and gather materials.
QUICKEST: Paper Plate Hand (p.142) or Rod (p.153) Puppet, Finger Puppet (p.136-138)
LONGER: Sock Hand Puppet (p.143), Wooden Spoon Rod Puppet (p.154)
FOCUS MATERIALS: unlined ½ file cards (or facsimile): about 10 /student, pencils, erasers, tape
3. **PRINT**
• Project Self Evaluation – one/student (p.44)

INTRODUCE

There are many ways to tell a story such as a book, a movie, a play, or puppet theater. Today we will learn a story from a book and you will re-tell this story using puppets that you will make. You will focus on just one scene, then we will put all the scenes together to tell the whole story in sequence, or from beginning to end.

READ ALOUD and DISCUSS the story: Who are the characters? Where does the story take place? What happened in the beginning, the middle, the end?

FOCUS (Day One)

1. Give each student two blank ½ file cards.
2. Instruct them to write on one "One day", and on the other, "The End".
3. Distribute one more card to each student. On this card, they will either write in words or draw what happened FIRST in the story just read.
4. Discuss what happened next, then distribute another card to draw that, and so on.
5. When finished (under ten cards total), ask the students to arrange their cards in sequence in front of them, "One day" at one end, and "The End" at the other. Number cards.
6. Tape the cards together, making a STORYBOARD (or accordion book).

REFLECT

You made a Storyboard: a series of drawings that show the events of a story. People who develop movies, picture books, or commercials start with a Storyboard. How would this help them?

CREATE (Day Two)

Each student makes puppets of the two characters, OR half the class makes one character, the other half makes the other.

REHEARSE (Day Two)

With students either at their desks, seated in a circle, or using a simple puppet stage, narrate the story with two students at a time manipulating their puppets to act out one scene at a time, possibly repeating important phrases after you, or adding improvised dialogue.
For example:
One day Hare and Tortoise decided to have a race. (students perform Scene One)
Hare raced ahead and Tortoise plodded slowly. (different students Scene Two)
Hare decided to take a nap because Tortoise was so far behind. (different students Scene Three), etc.
Change to a different pair of students for each scene, so that the story is told in sequence.
Re-tell the story, gradually allowing the students to direct the sequence.
Encourage students to use movement to show action and emotion, and to give their puppets an expressive voice to improvise dialogue.

OPTIONAL (especially for large class): Add Sound Effects Orchestra (p.172) pairing a puppeteer and a musician for each character and scene.

SHARE

Perform whole-class sequential presentation:
- for another class
- for a segment of the school community, such as parents.

REFLECT

You just accomplished a lot! You learned a story, made a storyboard, made puppets, and performed the story for ____! Did you have a favorite part of the project? What did you learn about what you are good at? What are some differences between sharing a story by reading it aloud, and using puppets? Is there anything you would do differently if you did a project with puppets again?

ASSESS

Teacher: Performance based
Students Grades K - 2: Self Evaluation: Collaborative Storytelling (p.44)

GRADES 3 - 5

ORGANIZE AND PREPARE

1. **SELECT** a puppet technique and gather materials:
QUICKEST: shadow (p.155) or simple sock (p.143)
LONGER: recycled or other head hand puppet (p.139), Toy Theater (p.162)
2. **PRINT**
* One copy/group **Story Planning Sheet** (p.43)
* **Project Checklist** for selected puppetry technique (Section IV) one/group
* Self Evaluation: Collaborative Storytelling one/student (p.45)
3. **DIVIDE CLASS** into groups of approximately 5 students and assign jobs:
THE RECORDER listens to all ideas and writes final decisions on the Story Planning Sheet.
THE CHECKLIST MANAGER checks off tasks on Project Checklist as they are finished.
THE MATERIALS CHIEF gathers any necessary materials for each step of the project and puts them away afterwards.
THE MODERATOR makes sure everyone has a chance to contribute ideas.
THE DIRECTOR observes the performance in rehearsal and makes suggestions for best communication with the puppets.
TIP: You may use stickers or paper slips on a string or safety pin as job ID's.
4. **ASK** Materials Chiefs to bring a pencil, a Story Planning Sheet and a Project Checklist to their groups.

INTRODUCE

You are beginning a project in which you will work in groups to write a story, create puppets, then perform for another class. First, you will use this Story Planning Sheet to help create your story. Your story will have only ONE main character. This character must have a problem that they have to somehow solve themselves by the end of the story. As you can see, there is very little space for writing on the sheet. You are to write only the main idea of what happens in the beginning, the middle, and the end – NOT every word the characters will speak, along with your title, setting, and characters. At the bottom is a list for your names and the puppet or prop you will make.

Each member of your group has a job to do:
The Recorder writes down the story everyone agrees to on the Story Planning Sheet.
The Checklist Manager checks off tasks on the Checklist as they are done.
The Materials Chief gathers and puts away necessary materials for each step of the project.
The Moderator makes sure that everyone has a chance to contribute ideas.
The Director watches the rehearsal to make suggestions for the best possible performance.
You MUST complete the Story Planning Sheet BEFORE beginning to make puppets.

FOCUS (Day One)

Groups collaborate to write a simple story sequence, using the Story Planning Page.

TIP: It helps to give groups a "story seed" around which to build the story, such as:
• an assigned topic
• a vocabulary list
• a "secret word" to inspire a place to start
* a prop (ONLY ONE)

Allow no more than 30 minutes for writing or students will write too much. NO extra paper is allowed.

ADVISEMENT: I have found that certain populations of children have a very hard time coming up with a story that is not resolved using violence or weapons. This resolution is forbidden in this project, and these children may need extra help.

My theory is that they are surrounded by stories of Good Guy vs. Bad Guy in cartoons, movies, even popular movie adaptations of traditional tales that did not start out that way. A great antidote is the reading of traditional folk and fairy tales, which have many different plot formats that people have invented for centuries – demonstrating that dominance by force is not necessarily the only way to approach a problem.

CREATE (Day One - Two)

Students build puppets and props as required for their story.

I am very strict that all story planning must be completed in writing BEFORE any puppet building materials are made available. Not only does this encourage a more focused team effort, but it also necessitates accomplishment of the core writing goals.

RATIONALE FOR SHORT WRITING FORMAT

In performance, the story dialogue is improvised because:

• The Planning Sheet is not allowed backstage, to allow total focus on puppet manipulation – impossible if reading at the same time.
• Improvisation during performance requires immediate response to character emotions and motivations and fosters acute listening, thinking, and response skills.
• Many classes include students with a spectrum of reading abilities so no script reading is required. Reading ability has no connection to creative thinking or performance skills.
• Script memorization takes time better spent on performance skills.

If you prefer complete scripts written and memorized, the Story Planning Page is still an effective place to begin.

The **Story Planning Page** facilitates:
• Construction of a cohesive story
• Agreement among group members on story events
• A written record of the group's plan, to be referred to and adhered to
• A simple framework on which improvised dialogue is based in performance

REHEARSE (Day Two)

Rehearse with group DIRECTORS.
Perform for class, including class Constructive Critique (p.171).

SHARE

Schedule a performance:
• for younger classes
• for classes doing the same project, to compare and contrast results
• for parents at an open house or other event
• if several classes participate, hold a Puppet Festival: an evening event with scheduled shows in different classrooms
TIP: Small audiences are best so that puppeteers' voices may be heard, unless amplification is available that does not necessitate leaning in to a microphone.

REFLECT

How was presenting a story with puppets different from presenting it as a writing project? How did your group work together to make sure everything needed was done? Do you have any tips for other groups about working collaboratively? Is there anything you would do differently if you did a project with puppets again?

ASSESS

Teacher: Performance based as well as Teamwork & Focus Rubric (p.170)
Student: Self Evaluation: Story Writing (p.45)

STORY PLANNING SHEET

PLOT: The events that happen in a story

The BEGINNING should answer the following questions:
Who is the ONE main character? Are there other characters they know? When and where does the story take place? What does the main character want?

The MIDDLE is the main conflict of the story.
What problem(s) keeps the main character from getting what they want?

The END resolves the conflict.
How does the main character succeed at getting what they want?

SETTING: Where does the story take place?

WHO is the MAIN CHARACTER?
WHO are the other characters?

TITLE: Title of your group's story

CONSTRUCTION PLAN: Who will make each puppet or prop?

Group Members' Names	Group Members' Jobs
1.	1.
2.	2.
3.	3.
4.	4.
5.	5.

Name _____ Date _____

How Did I Do?
COLLABORATIVE STORYTELLING: Grades K - 2

Circle the number of stars that you think best describe your work for each question.

AS A THINKER
1. I read or listened to the story and helped decide the most important scenes.

    *   ***   *****

2. I read or listened to the story and helped list the scenes in story sequence.

    *   ***   *****

AS AN ART MAKER
3. I made a puppet for the character or scene I was assigned.

    *   ***   *****

AS A PERFORMER:
4. I cooperated with my group to use my puppet to tell my part of the story.

    *   ***   *****

5. I held my puppet so that the audience could see its face.

    *   ***   *****

6. I gave my puppet expressive movement showing action and emotion.

    *   ***   *****

AS AN AUDIENCE MEMBER:
7. I watched each performance quietly.

    *   ***   *****

8. I was polite and thoughtful in my comments about others performances.

    *   ***   *****

---

9. My thoughts on the experience (use back of paper if needed):

Name _____ Date _____

How Did I Do?
COLLABORATIVE STORY WRITING: Grades 3 - 5

AS A WRITER
1. I contributed ideas to my team's story.

       *   ***   *****

2. I worked with my team to complete the Story Sheet.

       *   ***   *****

3. I worked with my team to write a story with a clear beginning, middle, and end.

       *   ***   *****

AS AN ART MAKER
4. I completed the puppet my team needed me to make for our story.

       *   ***   *****

AS A PERFORMER
5. I cooperated with my team to tell the story we had created.

       *   ***   *****

6. I moved my puppet with purpose to show action and speaking and made sure it faced the audience.

       *   ***   *****

7. I took the performance seriously and did my best to bring our story to life.

       *   ***   *****

8. I listened to the critique.

       *   ***   *****

AS AN AUDIENCE MEMBER
9. I watched the shows quietly.

       *   ***   *****

10. I gave polite and thoughtful comments in critique.

       *   ***   *****

_____

11. My thoughts on the experience (use back of paper if needed):

PROJECT FIVE: PERK UP THE PLOT!
Driving Question: How can we write a story with dynamic structure?

Grades: 3 – 5

Overview
Students create puppets and use a story template to create collaborative shadow puppet skits demonstrating dynamic story structure.
Time: Two 45 minute classes

Core Standards: Language Arts:
Writing: Text Types and Purposes;
Production of Writing
Speaking and Listening:
Comprehension and Collaboration;
Presentation of Knowledge and Ideas

ORGANIZE AND PREPARE

1. **SELECT** a puppet technique and gather materials.
QUICKEST: Shadow Puppets (p.155)
LONGER: any
2. **PRINT**
• Story Template Page (one per two students) (p.48)
• Project Checklist for selected puppetry technique (Section IV)
• Project Self Evaluation – one/student (p.49)
• Teamwork & Focus Rubric (p.170)

Expected Learning Outcomes:
Students will be able to create an expressive puppet character.
Students will be able to analyze plot structure as they create a story using a plot template.
Students will be able to evaluate and explain the result of thoughtful plot structure on story writing.

INTRODUCE Project Arc

We are beginning a project to construct and perform a story with a dynamic, or interesting, plot structure. You will first make puppets. Then you will work with a partner to write a story featuring the puppet characters you made. You will use a template to help you take a simple idea to an exciting story. Then you will perform your stories with the puppets.

CREATE (Day One)
Students construct a puppet in a form of their choice.

INTRODUCE Task

Now that your puppets are made, you will work with a partner to write a story for your two puppets. You are going to use a Plot Template with some of the words already written to help you create a strong story framework for your puppets. A story that goes, "A girl wanted a pet and she got it. The End", is not much of a story. A story needs conflict, or a problem to solve, to be interesting. We need to know there is something the main character wants very much, and they should have several problems to solve before they get what they want. And they may not get exactly what they thought they wanted in the beginning, but may learn something along the way that leads them to a different satisfactory

VOCABULARY:

Plot template: a framework within which to build a story

Critique: thoughtful comments on the work of someone else

ending. Notice that the Plot Template includes a #1 and a #2 version. Fill out both of these using the same story idea and be able to explain the difference.

CREATE (Day One - Two)
Working in groups of two, students collaborate to write stories featuring their puppet characters using the plot template.
• If any VERY simple puppet props are needed in the story, make them now.

REHEARSE
Each team selects a student not in their group as narrator to stand next to the shadow screen and read the story aloud.
The narrator must read slowly and also watch the screen to match the story to the action and allow time for the puppets' movements.
Students perform work for the class, with class Constructive Critique (p.171).

SHARE (Day Two)
Each team presents both story versions to a younger class.
After performance of each story pair, audience is asked which one they liked better and why.

REFLECT
How did the Plot Template affect your story writing?
How could you use what you learned now without the template?
How did hearing feedback from your audience affect your thinking about your work?

ASSESS
Teacher: Performance based as well as Teamwork & Focus Rubric (p.170)
Student: Self Evaluation: Template (p. 49)

PLOT TEMPLATE

_____
(TITLE)

Written by: _____ and _____

PLOT # 1: _____wanted _____ and that happened. THE END.
       (NAME OF MAIN CHARACTER?)   (WHAT?)

PLOT # 2: _____ was a _____ who
       (NAME OF MAIN CHARACTER?)   (WHO/WHAT?)

lived _____ .
        (WHERE?)

One day, _____ wanted_____ .
        (MAIN CHARACTER)   (WHAT?)

But he/she had a problem because _____ .
              (WHY?)

_____ tried to _____
     (MAIN CHARACTER)   (DO WHAT TO REACH GOAL?)

but _____ .
       (WHAT HAPPENED THAT FAILED?)

So _____ decided to _____
     (MAIN CHARACTER)   (TRY SOMETHING ELSE)

but then _____, and _____
      (WHAT HAPPENED THAT FAILED?)   (MAIN CHARACTER)

was ready to give up.

Finally, _____ tried _____
      (MAIN CHARACTER)   (WHAT?)

and _____ and _____was happy.
   (WHAT HAPPENED THAT SUCCEEDED?)   (MAIN CHARACTER)

Name _____ Date _____

How Did I Do?
TEMPLATE TO PERFORMANCE

AS AN ART MAKER
1. I completed my puppet.

      *   ***   *****

AS A WRITER
2. I shared ideas with my partner to write a story with the Plot Template.

      *   ***   *****

3. We chose one puppet to be the main character and made sure to write a part for the other puppet as well.

      *   ***   *****

4. We filled in every space in the template with a single word or very short phrase to complete the sentence.

      *   ***   *****

AS A PERFORMER
5. I held my puppet flat against the shadow screen, grasping the rod at the far end to make a sharp shadow with minimal shadow of my hand.

      *   ***   *****

6. I moved my puppet with purpose to show action and speaking.

      *   ***   *****

7. I took the performance seriously and did my best to bring our story to life.

      *   ***   *****

8. I listened to the critique.

      *   ***   *****

AS AN AUDIENCE MEMBER
9. I watched the shows quietly.

      *   ***   *****

10. I gave polite and thoughtful comments in critique.

      *   ***   *****

_____

11. My thoughts on the experience (use back of paper if needed):

LESSON SIX: FROM WOLF TO SHARK
Driving Question: How do writers give an old story a fresh start?

Grades: 3 – 5

Overview
Students collaborate to adapt a familiar tale to a new setting and characters, then build puppets to perform their story.
Time: Two or more 45 minute classes (depending on puppet technique)

Core Standards: Language Arts:
Writing: Text Types and Purposes; Production of Writing

Speaking and Listening: Comprehension and Collaboration;
Presentation of Knowledge and Ideas

ORGANIZE AND PREPARE

1. **SELECT** a puppet technique and gather materials.
QUICKEST: Shadow, Tabletop (including found object)
LONGER: Hand, Rod, or Toy Theater
2. **PRINT** one of each per group:
• Story Planning Sheet (p.54)
• Story Adaptation Plan (p.53)
• Project Checklist for selected Puppetry Technique (Section IV)
• Project Self Evaluation – one/student (p.55)
• Teamwork & Focus Rubric (p.170)
3. **SELECT** a story to analyze with the class. Suggested are simple, familiar folktales or fables with universal themes that can be re-imagined in different settings such as: The Fisherman and His Wife, The Frog Prince, The Boy Who

Expected Learning Outcomes:
Students will be able to recognize the interrelationship between plot, characters, and setting in a story.
Students will be able to rewrite a story as an adaptation.
Students will be able to design and create puppets to tell a story written in collaboration.

Cried Wolf, The Lion and the Mouse, etc. *With younger children, or those experiencing this activity for the first time, it is recommended that all work with the same story, but write their own adaptations.*
4. **DIVIDE CLASS** into groups of 3 - 5 students and assign jobs (some may have more than one job if small groups):
The Recorder listens to all ideas and writes final decisions on the Story Planning Sheet.
The Checklist Manager checks off tasks on Project Checklist as they are finished.
The Materials Chief gathers any necessary materials for each step of the project and puts them away afterwards.
The **Moderator** makes sure everyone has a chance to contribute ideas.
The **Director** observes the performance in rehearsal and makes suggestions for improved communication with the puppets.
5. **ASK** Materials Chiefs to bring a pencil, a Story Adaptation Plan, a Story Planning Sheet, and a Project Checklist to their groups.

VOCABULARY:

Setting: where and when the story takes place

Characters: who the story is about

Plot: the events that happen in the story

Adapt: to adjust or change for different conditions or situations

Character traits: unique qualities that make one character differ from another

INTRODUCE

Every story has three essential parts: the plot, the characters, and the setting. An adaptation of a story happens when one or more of those three elements is changed. For example, what if the setting of The Three Little Pigs was changed to underwater? The adaptation might feature three little fish and a big, bad shark. Or what if the famous race between the Tortoise and the Hare was adapted to the soccer field, and the competition was between a star player and a hardworking beginner? The story remains the same – only the setting and characters change. We will read a story and you will work in groups to create your own adaptation of this story, then bring your story to life with puppets.

You must complete the Story Adaptation Plan and Story Planning Sheet before beginning to make puppets.

FOCUS

1. Read story aloud to class. Discuss and list character traits of three main characters.

2. Each group completes a Story Adaptation Plan. *Emphasize that the plot will remain the same – only the setting and characters will change.*

3. Each group completes a Story Planning Sheet for their story.

CREATE (Class two, or more if needed)

Build puppets and essential props.

REHEARSE

Rehearse with group DIRECTORS.

Perform for class, including class Constructive Critique.

SHARE

Schedule a performance:

• for younger classes

RECOMMENDED: Provide younger audiences with a copy of the original tale to read before seeing the adaptation.

• with classes doing the same project, to compare and contrast results

• for parents at an open house or other event

• if several classes participate, hold a Puppet Festival: an evening event with scheduled shows in different classrooms

TIP: Small audiences are best so that puppeteers' voices may be heard, unless amplification is available that does not necessitate leaning in to a microphone.

RATIONALE FOR SHORT WRITING FORMAT

In performance, the story dialogue is improvised because:

• The Planning Sheet is not allowed backstage, to allow total focus on puppet manipulation – impossible if reading at the same time.

• Improvisation during performance requires immediate response to character emotions and motivations and fosters acute listening, thinking, and response skills.

• Many classes include students with a spectrum of reading abilities so no script reading is required. Reading ability has no connection to creative thinking or performance skills.

• Script memorization takes time better spent on performance skills.

If you prefer complete scripts written and memorized, the Story Planning Page is still an effective place to begin.

The **Story Planning Page** facilitates:

• Construction of a cohesive story

• Agreement among group members on story events

• A written record of the group's plan, to be referred to and adhered to

• A simple framework on which improvised dialogue is based in performance

REFLECT

How did changing the characters affect your setting, or changing your setting affect your characters? What elements of the original story did you recognize when watching the adaptations?

ASSESS

Teacher: Performance based as well as Teamwork & Focus Rubric (p.170)
Student: Self Evaluation: Story Adaptation (p.55)

a lost child

a dark forest

a stormy ocean

another galaxy

a clever rabbit

long, long ago

a little pink fish

a space explorer

STORY ADAPTATION PLAN

TEAM MEMBERS NAMES:

ORIGINAL STORY

TITLE: _____

SETTING: _____

ORIGINAL MAIN CHARACTERS' NAMES:

1. _____ 2. _____ 3. _____

CHARACTER TRAITS FOR BOTH STORIES' CHARACTERS:

1. _____ 2. _____ 3. _____

1. _____ 2. _____ 3. _____

1. _____ 2. _____ 3. _____

1. _____ 2. _____ 3. _____

1. _____ 2. _____ 3. _____

NEW STORY

NEW MAIN CHARACTERS' NAMES:

1. _____ 2. _____ 3. _____

NEW SETTING: _____

NEW TITLE: _____

STORY PLANNING SHEET

PLOT: The events that happen in a story

The BEGINNING should answer the following questions:
Who is the ONE main character? Are there other characters they know? When and where does the story take place? What does the main character want?

The MIDDLE is the main conflict of the story.
What problems keep the main character from getting what they want?

The END resolves the conflict.
How does the main character succeed at getting what they want?

SETTING: Where does the story take place?

WHO is the MAIN CHARACTER?
WHO are the other characters?

TITLE: Title of your group's story

CONSTRUCTION PLAN: Who will make each puppet or prop?

Group Members' Names	Group Members' Jobs
1.	1.
2.	2.
3.	3.
4.	4.
5.	5.

Name _____ Date _____

How Did I Do?
STORY ADAPTATION

AS A WRITER
1. I contributed to my team's story adaptation in changing the setting and characters.

*   ***   *****

2. I worked with my team to complete the Story Adaptation Sheet.

*   ***   *****

3. I worked with my team to complete the Story Planning Sheet with a clear beginning, middle, and end.

*   ***   *****

AS AN ART MAKER
4. I completed the puppet my team needed me to make for our story.

*   ***   *****

AS A PERFORMER
5. I cooperated with my team to tell the story we had created.

*   ***   *****

6. I moved my puppet with purpose to show action and speaking and made sure it faced the audience.

*   ***   *****

7. I took the performance seriously and did my best to bring our story to life.

*   ***   *****

8. I listened to the critique.

*   ***   *****

AS AN AUDIENCE MEMBER
9. I watched the shows quietly.

*   ***   *****

10. I gave polite and thoughtful comments in critique.

*   ***   *****

_____

11. My thoughts on the experience (use back of paper if needed):

PROJECT SEVEN: PUPPETS AND POETRY
Driving Question: How can words become pictures?

Grades: K - 2, 3 - 5

Overview
Students respond to poetry by creating visual imagery to accompany a reading of the poem.

Grades Kindergarten through Second listen to the text of a poem to find concrete or abstract elements to make visual as puppets to accompany a reading of the poem.

Grades Three through Five analyze poems and plan using a storyboard, sequential images to dramatize a reading of the poem.

CORE STANDARDS: LANGUAGE ARTS:
Reading: Key Ideas and Details; Craft and Structure; Integration of Knowledge and Ideas
Speaking and Listening: Comprehension and Collaboration; Presentation of Knowledge and Ideas

EXPECTED LEARNING OUTCOMES:
Students will be able to analyze the language of a poem for direct and inferred ideas and imagery.
Students will be able to integrate implied or inventive imagery into a poem as visual elements.
Students will be able to dramatize text with added visual imagery and purposeful movement.

GRADES K – 2
TIME: One 45 minute class session

ORGANIZE AND PREPARE
1. **SELECT** a puppet technique and gather materials.
QUICKEST: Rod: Paper shapes (p.147)
LONGER: Toy Theater (p.162)
2. **SELECT** a poem that includes open-ended visual imagery (poems of: Langston Hughes highly recommended, also Eloise Greenfield, Shel Silverstein, Jack Prelutsky).

INTRODUCE
A poem is a piece of writing that often has words that make you think of pictures in your mind. I am going to read a poem to you. As you listen, think of the pictures the poem makes you think of. Then, after the poem, you will tell me what pictures you imagined. I will look for everyone to be able to add something different. Then, you will share the picture in your mind with everyone by making a puppet of it.

VOCABULARY:

Poem: a piece of writing that usually has figurative language and is written in separate lines which may have a repeated rhythm and sometimes rhyme

Imagery: language that causes people to imagine pictures in their mind

FOCUS
1. Read and discuss poem as a class.
2. Ask students to state images they saw in their minds from the poem including Objects, People, Animals, Colors, Weather, Moods, etc.
3. List images with student name as they are stated, encouraging each student to think of something different.

CREATE

Each student makes a simple puppet of their image idea.
SUGGESTION for rod puppets: Add very lightweight materials that give movement either to the puppet, or to the rod immediately below the puppet: plastic tape ribbon (from hardware store), feathers, paper strips, shredded plastic grocery bags in various colors.

REHEARSE

With a narrator reading the poem slowly, ask students to move their puppet to accompany the words that inspired their image.

SHARE

Schedule a performance:
• for other classes
• for classes doing the same project, to compare and contrast results
• for parents at an open house or other event
• if several classes participate, hold a Poetry Festival.
If the puppets made are not too small, this project may be presented to a larger audience as the narrator may use a microphone.
TIP: Sound effects may accompany the presentation. See Sound Effects Orchestra (p.166).

REFLECT

The next time you read a poem, what might you look for in the words?

ASSESS

Performance based

GRADES 3 - 5

TIME: One - two 45 minute class sessions, depending on puppet technique selected.

ORGANIZE AND PREPARE

1. **SELECT** a puppet technique and gather materials.
QUICKEST: Shadow,(p.155), Rod: Paper shapes (p.153)
LONGER: Toy Theater (p.162), Parade Puppets (p.150)
For a large-scale presentation, Parade Puppets can make a powerful statement, depicting people, natural elements of the Earth and nature.
2. **SELECT** and **PRINT** on separate sheets a selection of poems that include metaphoric and open-ended imagery (poems of: Langston Hughes highly recommended, also Eloise Greenfield, Shel Silverstein, Jack Prelutsky).
3. **PRINT** one of each per group:
• Poetry Planning Sheet (p.59)
• Poetry Planning Storyboard (p.60)
• Self Evaluation: Poetry – one/student (p.61)
• Teamwork & Focus Rubric (p.170)
4. **FORM** groups of 3 – 5 students.

INTRODUCE

A poem is a piece of writing that often contains language that causes people to imagine pictures in their mind. These pictures in your mind are called imagery. We are going to find imagery in poetry, and actually make those pictures in your mind visible with puppets. You may have pictures in your mind of inferred imagery – in other words, images or emotions that are not directly stated, but that you see or feel anyway. These ideas can be puppets as well.

FOCUS

1. Read and discuss a sample poem as a class, listing images students saw in their minds from the poem's text, either literal or inferred.
2. Assign, or allow groups to choose, a poem or stanza to work with.
3. Each group reads their poem and each member fills out a Poetry Planning Page.
4. Members share the ideas from their Planning Page.
5. Each group plans a sequence of images and makes VERY quick sketches in the Poetry Storyboard. *Remember that the puppets may be shapes representing objects, natural elements of the Earth and nature, elements of a particular environment, emotions – NOT necessary people or animals.*

CREATE

Groups construct puppets.

REHEARSE

1. Practice presenting the poem along with imagery. As the poem is read (slowly, to accommodate visual scenes), students accompany text, as well as spaces between text lines, with appropriate movement of their puppets. A narrator may read the poem while puppeteers manipulate the puppets, OR each puppeteer may say the line of the poem that accompanies their puppet image.
2. Perform for class, including class Constructive Critique.

SHARE

Schedule a performance:
• for other classes
• for classes doing the same project, to compare and contrast results
• for parents at an open house or other event
• if several classes participate, hold a Poetry Festival.
If the puppets made are not too small, this project may be presented to a larger audience as the narrator may use a microphone.
TIP: Sound effects may accompany the presentation. See Sound Effects Orchestra (p.166).

REFLECT

The next time you read a poem, what might you look for in the words?

ASSESS

Teacher: Performance based as well as Teamwork & Focus Rubric (p.164)
Student: Self Evaluation: Poetry (p.61)

Poetry Planning Sheet

Group members: _____

Poem title: _____

by: _____

1. What is the poem about?

2. What emotion(s) do you feel from this poem?

3. What color(s) would you chose to represent this poem? State a reason for each color.

4. What sound(s) would you chose to represent this poem? State a reason for each sound.

5. What images NOT stated in the poem text, does it make you think of?

Use back (and additional paper if needed) for:
6. What real life event(s) does the poem make you think of – either general or from a specific personal memory?

NEXT STEP: With your team, create a sequence using concrete (people, things) and/or abstract (shapes, colors) images to perform with a reading of the poem. Working together, make a STORYBOARD of your plan using the POETRY STORYBOARD page. Write the line from the poem under each box and make a quick sketch of your planned puppet imagery in the box.

Group members: ____________________

POETRY PLANNING STORYBOARD

SCENE 1

SCENE 2

SCENE 3

SCENE 4

SCENE 5

SCENE 6

SCENE 7

SCENE 8

SCENE 9

Name _____ Date _____

How Did I Do?
POETRY AND PUPPETRY

AS A THINKER
1. I listened to the text of a poem for the pictures it created in my mind.

      *   ***   *****

2. I completed the Poetry Planning Sheet.

      *   ***   *****

3. I worked with my team to complete the Poetry Storyboard Sheet.

      *   ***   *****

AS AN ART MAKER
4. I completed the puppet my team needed me to make for our plan.

      *   ***   *****

AS A PERFORMER
5. I cooperated with my team to present the work we had created.

      *   ***   *****

6. I listened to the poem text and moved my puppet with purpose.

      *   ***   *****

7. I took the performance seriously and did my best to bring our story to life.

      *   ***   *****

8. I listened to the critique.

      *   ***   *****

AS AN AUDIENCE MEMBER
9. I watched the shows quietly.

      *   ***   *****

10. I gave polite and thoughtful comments in critique.

      *   ***   *****

_____

11. My thoughts on the experience (use back of paper if needed):

PROJECT SERIES EIGHT: KEYS TO READING
Driving Question: What is our brain actually doing when we read?

Grades: K - 2
Time: Series of eight 30-45 minute classes
Overview: Students create a series of simple puppets to become conscious of reading comprehension skills: making connections, questioning, visualizing, inferring, determining importance, and synthesizing. Each of the eight lessons includes the construction and use of a very simple puppet which serves as an imaginative connection to make each point memorable. Some puppet designs are not in the puppet making section and are within these lessons. Each lesson is a self contained unit, connected in theme to the others. A culminating sharing project ties the lessons together.

CORE STANDARDS: LANGUAGE ARTS
Reading: Key Ideas and Details; Craft and Structure;
Integration of Knowledge and Ideas
Speaking and Listening: Presentation of Knowledge and Ideas

EXPECTED LEARNING OUTCOMES:
Students will be able to differentiate specific skills needed for reading.
Students will be able to demonstrate reading comprehension skills through the use of puppets.
Students will be able to design and perform with a variety of puppet techniques.

INTRODUCE Project Arc

Reading is an amazing and useful skill that we can master. Master means work to be very good at. We can work at understanding what we read by using a few specific skills – like clues to help us get inside the meaning of the words and sentences. We will start a series of lessons now, working with puppets to help us understand the meaning of what we read.

VOCABULARY:
Connection: something that joins two or more things together

Question: a sentence that asks for information

Visualize: to see in your mind

Infer: to reach your own conclusion based on facts

Determine importance: to analyze for most and least significant elements

Synthesize: to combine different things in order to make something new

CLASS ONE: Reading Buddy Bookworm!
Driving Question: What is Text?

ORGANIZE AND PREPARE
1. **POST** in classroom examples of TEXT (books, magazines, signs, maps, food boxes, instructions, etc.)
2. **GATHER** Puppet Making Materials:
craft sticks (or cardboard or sturdy paper strips)
markers or crayons
OPTIONAL: small wiggly eyes & glue
3. **PRINT**
• Project Self Evaluation (p.73) one/student

FOCUS
We use words to talk and communicate with each other. When we write these words down, they are called TEXT. There is text all around us every day. Point to some text you see in this room. (Show craft stick puppet) This is my Reading Buddy, Bookworm. He loves to find text and have me read to him

what it says. You are each going to make your own Reading Buddy Bookworm today.

CREATE
Students make Bookworm Puppets by gluing (or drawing) eyes on one end of the craft stick and decorating the stick with markers.

SHARE
Working independently or in pairs, students explore with their puppet to locate and read displayed text.

REFLECT
What samples of text did your Bookworms find? What was the purpose of the text they found?

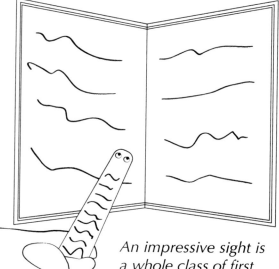

An impressive sight is a whole class of first graders exploring for text to read to their craft-stick bookworms.

CLASS TWO: Putting Thinky To Work!
Driving Question: How is our brain connected to reading?

ORGANIZE AND PREPARE
1. **GATHER** Puppet Making Materials:
one grey sock OR small paper bag per student
markers, crayons, or paint
OPTIONAL: medium wiggly eyes & glue
one or two plastic grocery bags per student
one completed Thinky Puppet for teacher.
These are extremely simple, almost abstract puppets, but effective for building awareness of conscious use of thinking skills, as well as making use of the child's vivid imagination as a learning tool.

FOCUS
When we read, we think. What part of our bodies do we use when we think? This is Thinky, my brain puppet. Thinky loves to figure out what the words mean when I read. Let's see how she does it.
Read aloud from a storybook with Thinky brain puppet as "thinking partner". Thinky makes comments after each page such as "I wonder what this book is about. I wonder what will happen next. I wonder why that character is wearing a big hat. etc."
You are each going to make your own Thinky Puppet.

CREATE
1. Using markers, quickly decorate toe end of sock or small paper bag with colorful designs.
2. Stuff plastic bags firmly inside.
3. Glue eyes on.

SHARE
1. Place hand inside sock or bag and grasp with thumb and opposing fingers to create a talking mouth (as sock mouth puppet p.143)
2. Each student and their Thinky work as "thinking partners" to make comments in a class reading of a picture book.

REFLECT
How does your brain help you read?

CLASS THREE: A Finger Puppet Me!
Driving Question: Can we connect what we read to our own life, or to other text?

ORGANIZE AND PREPARE
SELECT a Finger Puppet technique (p.136-137) and gather materials.
SELECT a picture book about a child in a common scenario. (as Whistle for Willie by Ezra Jack Keats)

FOCUS
When you read, your brain is working to make connections from the text to your real life experiences, or to other text you have read. This helps you to understand what is going on in the text or story. You are going to make a little puppet of yourself to help make connections to reading.

CREATE
Make "Self" Finger puppets

SHARE
Read selected story aloud. Each puppet is given an opportunity to tell of a personal experience the story reminded them of. Remind students this is a puppet of them, so the puppet will speak in the first person ("This story reminds me of when I…")

REFLECT
Did your puppets do a good job of telling what the text reminded them of? Can you think of any book or movie the text reminded you of?

CLASS FOUR: Draw What You Imagine!
Driving Question: How does reading make us see pictures in our mind?

ORGANIZE AND PREPARE
1. SELECT a book with an undefined main character, such as in <u>Who's In Rabbit's House?</u> by Verna Ardeema, <u>My Teacher is a Monster,</u> by Peter Brown, <u>The Adventures of Beekle,</u> by David Santat, <u>The Dark</u>, by Lemony Snicket.
2. GATHER Puppet Making Materials:
one sheet approx. 8.5 x11 heavy paper/child

pencils, crayons or markers
scissors, tape
one popsicle stick/child

FOCUS

When you read, your mind is forming pictures of what the text describes. This is called visualizing. Seeing these pictures in your mind helps you to understand the meaning of the text. We are going to find out how hard your brain works at visualizing.
READ selected book aloud WITHOUT SHOWING PICTURES. Stop reading before any description of the character is made.

CREATE

Ask students to make a PAGE-SIZED (not tiny) picture of how they imagined this character. Students cut out their character and tape a stick to the top as a control rod.

SHARE

On table or desk top, each puppet tells something about itself, as related to the story.

REFLECT

Was everyone's picture the same? No, because we all used our imagination and visualized something different.
Can you describe in words why your imagination saw the character the way you drew it?

CLASS FIVE: Whose Luggage?
Driving Question: How does inferring, or finding clues, help us understand what we read?

ORGANIZE AND PREPARE

1. **GATHER** Puppet Making Materials:
Same as Class Four
2. **PRINT** one set of Lost Luggage (p.70, 71, 72)
3. **CUT** in segments and **FOLD** each section with text on the inside.

FOCUS

When we read, we find clues to explain things that may not be directly in the text. This is called inferring. When you infer meaning in a text, you might say I think… , or It could be that… , or maybe… . For example, the text might say, "Diamond has a furry pet." You know there are lots of furry pet possibilities, but when the text says, "Her pet barked loudly." you might infer that her pet is a dog.
You are about to receive some clues to create a character. You see, an airline lost all the luggage, or suitcases, for a whole plane full of passnegers. The airline needs you to help figure out who each suitcase belongs to. You will each have a suitcase to open. You will see what is in the sutcase and try to figure out, or infer, from what you find in the suitcase. Everyone will have a different suitcase. Then, as in the last lesson, you will make a large drawing of that person to make into a puppet.

CREATE
1. Each student receives their suitcase to examine. Advise to keep the contents a SECRET!
2. Each student makes large drawing of who they think the suitcase belongs to.
3. Color and cut out the character, and attach control stick at top.

SHARE
Each student first shares their suitcase with the class, and listens to class' ideas on the owner. Then, student's puppet enters and explains why it is their suitcase and how they use the items. There may be more than one idea for some suitcases so students must explain how they inferred their decision.

REFLECT
How did you use the skill of inferring in figuring out who lost the luggage?
How could you use this skill in the next book you read?

HINTS*: Here are my answers for the secret luggage, but there may be other ideas: rabbit, lion, puppy, zoo keeper, chef, crossing guard, witch, clown, farmer, snowman, cow, PE teacher, landscape painter, immigrant builder, grandma, pizza deliverer, cat, cowboy, undersea explorer, frog, fireman, singer, bear, fairy, T-Rex, runner, doctor.*

CLASS SIX: Shadow Magic
Driving Question: How do you decide what is most important in what you read?

ORGANIZE AND PREPARE
1. **GATHER** Puppet Making Materials:
Shadow Puppets (p.155)
PRE-CUT black paper so that each child receives one larger and one smaller piece
2. **SELECT** an engaging and not overly simple illustrated book.

FOCUS
When we read, we need to be able to tell apart the most important characters and events from those that are not so important.
We will read a story and you will make quick puppets of one important and one less important character or other thing in the story, so be thinking about this as you listen.
READ story of your choice, discussing what is most and least important on each page.

CREATE
On this large paper, you will make a large drawing of something important in the story, then cut it out. (Complete before giving second piece of paper.)
Now, on this smaller paper, you will make a drawing of something less important in the story and also cut it out.

Attach control rods as directed (p.155).

SHARE
The puppets introduce themselves in the first person to tell why they are important, or not, in the story.

REFLECT
How did you decide what to choose as most or least important for your puppets?

CLASS SEVEN: Curious Critters
Driving Question: How does thinking of questions help us understand what we read?

ORGANIZE AND PREPARE
1. **SELECT** a puppet technique and gather materials.
   QUICKEST: Rod or Hand Puppets: Paper Plate (p.142 or 153)
   LONGER: simple sock Hand Puppets (p.143)
2. **SELECT** an engaging picture book.

FOCUS
When we read, we think of questions we have about the characters, setting, and events of the story. These questions may be answered as we continue reading the story. We will make puppets that are curious – they want to ask all kinds of questions about what we read.

CREATE
Make Curious Critter puppets.

SHARE
READ selected picture book, allowing puppets to take turns asking questions about each page.

REFLECT
How did examining each page with your curious puppet help you find more interesting details in the story?

CLASS EIGHT: A Story In A Cup
Driving Question: How do we bring together all our tools - or synthesize - when we read?

ORGANIZE AND PREPARE
1. **SELECT** a puppet technique and gather materials.
QUICKEST: Paper Cup Theater: very small paper rod puppets can appear from inside a paper cup with a hole in the bottom to perform for a very small audience.
MATERIALS per theater:
one paper (**NOT** stirofoam or plastic) cup, hole pre-cut in bottom

three straws or thin skewers
paper scraps, tape, colored pencils or markers
TO MAKE:
1. Draw or collage on small paper shapes to make two or three characters.
2. Tape to end of straw or thin skewer.
3. Insert rods through hole in cup.
4. Allow characters to enter and exit from inside cup to tell story.
LONGER: Toy Theater: Mini Toy Theater (p.162)
2. **SELECT** stories with only two or three main characters: Aesop's Fables, The Paper Bag Princess, by Robert Munsch

FOCUS
When you use synthesizing as you read, you are bringing together all your tools to understand what you are reading. You will make puppets to tell a story by yourself in your own little puppet stage. So, you will have to make decisions about what the characters look like, what they say, which ones are most important and you can do this by finding clues in the text.
1. **READ** aloud simple, familiar folktales, fairytales, or Aesop fables with no more than two or three characters.

CREATE
1. Each student selects their own story, OR all work with the same story, depending on age and focus of students.
2. Each student either writes or makes a quick drawsing of the necessary characters.
3. Make puppets.

SHARE
Perform stories for each other in classroom setting.

REFLECT
Allow opportunity for positive comments from the class after each show.
You just accomplished a lot! You told a story you learned using puppets you made and you decided what the characters would say.
Did this story remind you of something that happened to you? Or of another story you have read?
When you saw the puppets, were they as you imagined the characters to look?
Was there anything you thought or figured out from clues in the story?
Who were the most important characters in the story? What was something that happened in the story that was not so important?
What questions did the story make you think of?

CULMINATION: SHARE WITH GREATER COMMUNITY
Allow students to connect and share what they learned with other classes and/or with parents
at a Reading Celebration event.

ORGANIZE AND PREPARE
Collect either 8 good sized boxes that can be opened out to form a puppet stage or 8 cardboard project boards
8 sheets of posterboard, or 8 large pieces of bulletin board paper
paint, markers, crayons or collage materials

CREATE
Students decorate posters featuring each of the focus areas:
Text is everywhere.
When we read, we think.
When we read, we make connections.
When we read, we determine importance.
When we read, we visualize.
When we read, we infer.
When we read, we think of questions.
When we read, we synthesize.

SHARE
Attach the posters to the front of the boxes or project boards, or to the wall spaced around a large space (library, hallway, gymnasium)
Station 2 – 3 students at each display with the puppets they made and books as needed to repeat the activity done with those puppets.
Invite visitors to tour so that the students can explain their focus point to them.

OR

SHARE AND ASSESS
Set up displays including sample puppets and books used and have students act as tour guides accompanying visitors to explain each point to them.

ASSESS
Teacher: Performance based
Student: Self Evaluation: Reading Comprehension (p.73)

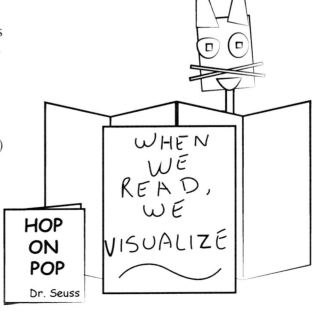

a carrot

a book:
How To Hide From a Fox

a very tall hat

---

a map of the jungle

a crown

a zebra steak recipe

---

a pillow bed

a chew toy

a plastic dish

---

some elephant food

some giraffe food

a book: Caring for Animals

---

a tall white hat

a cookbook

a large spoon

---

a bright colored vest

a stop sign

a whistle

---

a book of magic

a pointy hat

a broom

---

some big purple shoes

a polka dot hat

balloons

---

a shovel

some seeds

a sun hat

red mittens

some sticks

a carrot

a top hat

---

some grass

a picture of a grassy field

a book: How I Turn Grass Into Milk

---

a basketball

a whistle

a school class schedule

---

a folding chair

a paintbrush

paper

mosquito repellant

---

a hammer

a house building plan

a Spanish/English dictionary

---

baby clothes

a note:
"Dear daughter, I can't wait to meet the new arrival!"

a fold-up rocking chair

---

a car key

a city map

a pizza box

---

a soft pillow

a toy mouse

a can of food

---

a saddle

a big hat

a lasso

a swim suit

a facemask and snorkel

a book: Fish of the Ocean

---

some flies

a poster:
Jumping Contest Rules

a lily pad

---

a heavy, waterproof
coat

a hose

a ladder

---

a microphone

a page of music with
lyrics to the song

a fancy costume

---

a very warm blanket

an alarm clock set to "Spring"

a book of bedtime stories

---

a bed made from flower petals

some magic dust

a wand

The All Dinosaur Meat Cookbook

meat

more meat

---

a stop watch

some running shoes

a bottle of water

---

some bandages

some medicine

a blanket

Name _____ Date _____

READING COMPREHENSION

AS A THINKER
1. I thought about each reading skill as a clue to get to the meaning of the text.

     *   ***   *****

2. I thought about what I wanted to show when I made my puppets.

     *   ***   *****

AS AN ART MAKER
3. I completed the puppet I needed for each part of the project.

     *   ***   *****

AS A PERFORMER

4. I moved my puppet with purpose to show when they were talking or doing something.

     *   ***   *****

5. I took the performance seriously and did my best to bring my story to life.

     *   ***   *****

6. I listened to the comments of my class and teacher about my performance.

     *   ***   *****

AS AN AUDIENCE MEMBER
7. I watched the shows quietly.

     *   ***   *****

8. I gave polite and thoughtful comments in critique.

     *   ***   *****

---

9. My thoughts on the experience (use back of paper if needed):

PROJECT SERIES NINE: PUPPET CITY
Driving Question: How does a community form and function?

Grades: 1 – 3
Overview: Based around landforms and basic human needs, students build and manage an interdependent community of puppets who trade goods and services, elect a mayor, and create cultural traditions.
Time: Ten 45 minute class sessions

CORE STANDARDS:
SOCIAL STUDIES:
Geography: Maps, Globes, and Environment
Civics: Government and Citizenship
Economics: Basic Economic Concepts
LANGUAGE ARTS:
Reading for Informational Text: Key Ideas and Details; Integration of Knowledge and Ideas
Speaking and Listening: Comprehension and Collaboration; Presentation of Knowledge and Ideas

EXPECTED LEARNING OUTCOMES:
Students will be able to recognize ways in which members of a community are interconnected.
Students will be able to apply learning in creative dramatics free play.
Students will be able to evaluate the effectiveness of a community based on how citizen needs are met.

VOCABULARY
(listed in order of use in the lessons):

community: a group of people living together
map: a representation of a physical place
map key: the symbols used to find places on a map
compass directions: North, South, East , or West
symbol: a picture or diagram used to stand for something else
natural land form: physical feature of the earth
man made form: something made by people
basic human needs: clean air and water, food, shelter, clothing
needs and wants: a need helps you stay alive, and a want is something you can live without
job: work people do for which they may be paid
goods: objects people want that they can touch or hold
services: an action that a person does for someone else
consumer: a person who buys goods and services
producer: someone or something that grows or makes particular goods or products
rule: a written statement that tells what is and is not allowed
election: a process allowing people to vote to select the winner
citizen: a member of a community
democracy: a type of government in which citizens vote to select their leaders
culture: the traditions and way of life of a particular group of people

CLASS ONE
Driving Question: What is a map?
ORGANIZE AND PREPARE
1. **GATHER** materials for Paper Walkers (p.138)
TIP: *Use the cut out window scrap from the buildings (Class Three), to make Paper Walkers!*
2. dry erase board and markers
PRINT
• Knowledge Quiz to measure learning at beginning and end of project – one/student (p.82)
• Project Self Evaluation – one/student (p.84)

INTRODUCE Project Arc
We will begin a unit today about what makes a community. A community is a group of people living together. Almost everyone lives in a community. We will find land for our community and build an actual community of puppets.

FOCUS
Today we start by working with a map. A map is a representation of a physical place.
OPTIONAL: Students complete Knowledge Quiz (p.82).

CREATE
Make Paper Walker Puppets. (Keep in classroom for next lesson).

SHARE
1. Collaborate with class to draw on dry erase board a simple map of the classroom, showing doors, windows, teacher desk, student desks, etc.
2. Students work with partner: One walks their puppet on the map while their partner must walk in the classroom where the puppet goes. Then reverse, so puppet must walk on the map where the student walks.

REFLECT
We made a map of our classroom and we read the map to find our way around. What else might people make maps of? Who might use these maps?

CLASS TWO
Driving Question: What can we learn from the map key?

ORGANIZE AND PREPARE
MATERIALS:
large world or other map with map key and compass rose
drawing paper
pencils
colored markers or pencils
Paper Walker Puppets from CLASS ONE
PRINT: One copy Map Landform Options and Community Roles (p.83)

FOCUS
Today we will examine a map of a real place then you will create a map of an imaginary place with landforms identified in a map key.
Observe and discuss a large map, referring to the map key and compass directions and identifying landforms on the map: mountain, river, ocean, island, forest, beach, desert, valley, etc.

CREATE
Each student draws a map of an imaginary place with a map key and labeled compass directions featuring at least five different natural landforms. Each map is titled (student's name)land.

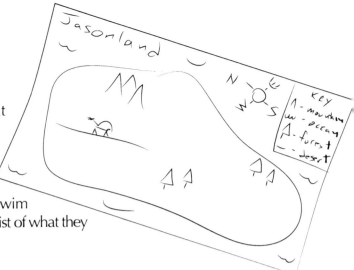

SHARE

1. Students trade maps with their neighbor so that their puppet may walk around and explore this new land, referring to the map key and compass directions.
2. Students decide what they need for their exploration of this land (a boat, climbing gear, a swim suit, a car, an airplane or helicopter, etc.) and make a list of what they need to bring for their trip.

REFLECT

How did the map key help you explore this map? What did the puppets enjoy most in their exploration? What were their favorite landforms? Why?

CLASS THREE
How does a community provide what people need to live?

ORGANIZE AND PREPARE

PRINT:
• One copy Community Role Options for reference, and to check off as taken (p.83)
• Community Connection Form: one/two students (then cut in half: p.84)
RECOMMENDED: Printed out list of class members – to record community roles.
MATERIALS:
file folders (may be recycled), with approximately 3" x 5" "window" pre-cut.
colored markers, crayons, or pencils

FOCUS

Basic needs all people need to live are clean air and water, food, clothing, and shelter. Additional needs are safety, health, education, recreation. These are things all communities should provide. Now that we have explored landforms, we will build a community of people (actually puppets) on our land. What would our puppets need in order to live here, to provide for their needs?

1. Discussion: It is helpful to write names and roles on board so students can see how the community grows. As students make suggestions, give them that "business" as their own – **so there is only one of each**. Build the businesses organically, for example:

Erin: They need houses.
Teacher: OK, you will own Erin's House Company. What will Erin need to build the houses?
Jeremy: She will need wood, hammers, nails.
Teacher: Good, you will own Jeremy's Building Supply Company. What else?
Jamahl: They need food.
Teacher: You will own Jamahl's Grocery Store. Where will Jamahl get the food to sell?
Freida: From a farm.
Teacher: Great – you will own Freida's Farm.

And so on, making sure all basic needs (including trash and recycling which should be spotlighted as a very important job) are met before adding beauty shops and dance studios, etc. Write each student's community role on the class sheet.

CREATE

Begin decorating storefronts: Folders are storefronts, with windows. At the top front, students make a decorative sign for the business, as "Student One's School" – so child's name is part of the business name. Students draw on their folder what they would see on the outside of the business, then turn the folder over to draw what would be found on the inside of the business.

REFLECT

Now our community will have what it needs. Why is your job important?

CLASS FOUR & FIVE
How do citizens in a community work together?

ORGANIZE AND PREPARE

1. **SELECT** puppet technique and gather materials:
Table Top: Wood Rod and Head, OR Bottle Buddies (p.160-161)
2. file folder buildings
3. colored markers

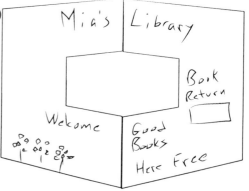

FOCUS

Today you will finish your buildings and make your puppet business owner. The puppet will have your name.

CREATE

1. **COMPLETE** decoration of inside and outside of file folders:
The outside will have signs and whatever else is seen on the outside of the building, and the other side shows what is inside the business. (For example the school: desks, students, teacher; the farm: cows, vegetables growing, etc.) *Encourage students to collaborate - for example, if the grocer wants to sell carrots, they should make sure the farmer grows carrots.*
2. **CONSTRUCT** puppets as community citizens.

SHARE

Set up community buildings, then invite each puppet to introduce itself, telling what its job is, and one other business it works closely with.

REFLECT

Can you name one other business you will need to work with?

CLASS SIX
What are goods and services?

ORGANIZE AND PREPARE

1. approximately 1" x 2" cardstock paper pieces, five per student. Use two different colors of paper, so that students whose business provides GOODS receive a different color from

those who provide SERVICES.
2. pencils
3. paper clips or sandwich bags to hold goods and services cards

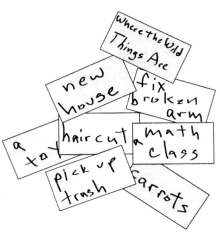

FOCUS

Businesses providing GOODS earn money selling things that people buy, such as food, clothing, etc. Businesses providing SERVICES earn money because of things they do for people, such as a doctor, teacher, police officer, barber, etc. Does your business provide goods or services?

If your business provides goods, you will receive 5 (color) cards. You will make a small picture on each card of something your business sells. If your business provides services, you will receive a (different color) card, and you will make a small drawing of a service you provide on each of your cards.

Make sure you think about what people need as well as what they want. Needs are what people have to have for a healthy life. Wants are things they may like but don't have to have to survuve.

What is an example of a NEED? What is an example of a WANT?

CREATE

1. Students make simple drawings on cards of goods or services each business provides.
2. Place cards in paper or sandwich bag pocket taped inside building folder.

SHARE

Allow time for a trading session, when puppet citizens may trade their cards, making sure to receive something their business needs, as well as something their puppet wants.
Explain that trading means they give a card and receive a card in return - so they end up with the same number of cards they started with, but all different cards made by other students.

REFLECT

When you trade goods and services rather than use money, this is called a barter system. People in our country use money, rather than barter, to get what we need. Did your puppet get what they need through bartering? How would a system using money work differently?

CLASS SEVEN
Why do communities need rules and laws?

ORGANIZE AND PREPARE

For teachers: dry erase board or facsimile, markers

FOCUS

Laws are necessary for safety and to make sure everyone is treated fairly. Today, we will write some laws, or rules, for our puppet citizens.

CREATE

Class together discusses and makes rules for the community including rules for behavior, which teacher writes down on board as laws.

SHARE

A visiting puppet news reporter (puppet operated by teacher) interviews each citizen, as all class watches, to ask what their role in the community is: who they do business with, what they need for their business, as well as something they want.
A free play period allows students to use all the concepts together, as they continue to trade goods and services, visit each other, etc.

REFLECT

Why are laws important? What is one thing your puppet learned about the community today?

CLASS EIGHT
What is a democracy?

ORGANIZE AND PREPARE
MATERIALS

Small paper slips as ballots, pencils.

FOCUS

A democracy is government of the people and by the people. In a democracy, the citizens vote for leaders who are responsible to do what they said they would do. Today we will elect a mayor of Puppetland. Our candidates, or people who are running for the office of mayor, will each give a short speech telling the citizens why they should vote for them. If your puppet would like to be mayor, they will give a speech saying why they deserve a vote. Everyone will think about each speech and then vote for the candidate they think will be the best mayor.

SHARE

1. Mayoral candidates give speeches.
3. Puppets vote by paper ballot. – primary and secondary election, if needed. The buildings are set up in front of each student as private voting booths.
4. The votes are counted.
5. Mayor gives thanks speech.

REFLECT

Why did you vote for the candidate you selected? Did the candidates make promises they could actually keep?

ORGANIZE AND PREPARE
MATERIALS
Misc. art materials: paper, fabric scraps, markers
CARDS each labeled with a different natural landform (as mountains, lake, river, beach)
CARDS each labeled with a different possible tradition (food, festival, dance, clothing, parade, game, etc.)

INTRODUCE
Culture is the way of life, customs, and beliefs of a particular group of people. Cultural traditions are also generally connected to the land where the people live. What cultural traditions happen in your community? These might be in food, celebrations, costume, dance, games, etc.

CREATE
1. Divide class into groups of 4-5 students.
2. Each group picks a tradition card and a landform card.
3. Each group creates a tradition of this type that reflects their geographic place of origin. (for example, a dance tradition from the people from the mountains, or a food tradition from the people who live by the ocean, etc.)
4. Each group creates simple props to present their tradition.

SHARE
Each group performs its cultural tradition for the other groups.

REFLECT
When you watched the presentations, how did the traditions reflect the landform they came from?

ORGANIZE AND PREPARE
OPTIONAL: PRINT second set of Knowledge Quiz (p.82).

FOCUS
You will take your puppets and buildings home today. This means the end of this community. In real life, events can happen so that a community can no longer survive. A large business that paid many of the people for their service might have to close and the people may have to leave to find other work. Or a flood or other natural disaster may make fixing all the buildings too big a job. Or a war may make the community too dangerous a place to live safely. What problems would people have if they no longer have a community?
OPTIONAL: Students re-take Knowledge Quiz

SHARE
Puppets say goodbye to each other, as are going home with puppeteers today.

REFLECT
What connections have you observed in your real community that you observed in the puppet community? Do you know where the food in your grocery store comes from? Did your parents vote for the mayor? For your own work when you grow up, would you like to provide goods or services? Why?

CULMINATION: SHARE WITH GREATER COMMUNITY

1. **WRITE**, in collaboration with class, a list of questions visitors might want to ask the puppets about their community, such as:
What is your job in the community?
Do you provide goods or services?
What are they?
Who do you work with most often in the community?
What are important laws in the community?
Who is the mayor?
Did you vote for this mayor? Why or why not?
2. **PRINT** these questions and duplicate for visitors.
3. **SET UP** puppet community on long table expanse, such as in cafeteria. Each student is seated with their puppet, behind their business.
4. **INVITE** visitors – other classes, or parents – to visit and ask questions about the community.

ASSESS
Teacher: Performance based
Student: Self Evaluation: Community (p.85)

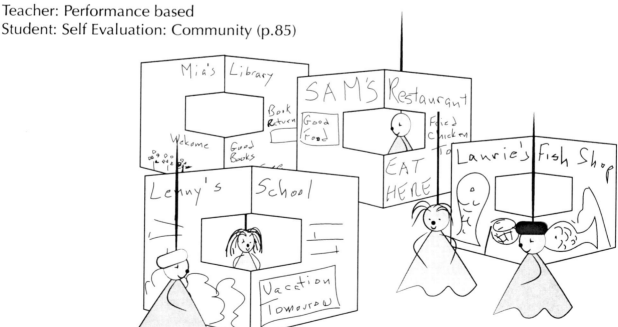

Knowledge Quiz

1. What is a map?
___A. A picture that shows the physical features of a certain place.
___B. A wall decoration.
___C. An island with palm trees.
___D. I don't know.

2. What is a map key used for?
___A. To find places on a map.
___B. To unlock a door.
___C. To keep a map inside.
___D. I don't know.

3. What is a symbol?
___A. A drawing.
___B. A simple picture used to stand for something else.
___C. A musical instrument
___D. I don't know.

4. Which of the following is a natural land form?
___A. a tall building
___B. a mountain
___C. a bridge
___D. I don't know.

5. Which of the following is a human, or man made, feature?
___A. an ocean
___B. a river
___C. a street
___D. I don't know

6. What are three basic human needs?
___A. food, clothing, and shelter
___B. friends, family, and a bed
___C. school, work, and play
___D. I don't know.

7. What does the word community mean?
___A. A place where people meet.
___B. A family.
___C. A group of people working together.
___D. I don't know.

8. What is the difference between needs and wants?
___A. There is no difference
___B. A need helps you stay alive, and a want is something you can live without.
___C. Wants you can buy at the store, and needs are free.
___D. I don't know.

9. Why do people have different jobs?
___A. To provide everything a community needs.
___B. For fun.
___C. So they don't get bored.
___D. I don't know.

10. Which of the following provides goods?
___A. a fire fighter
___B. a grocery store
___C. a doctor
___D. I don't know.

11. Which of the following provides services?
___A. a restaurant
___B. a teacher
___C. a toy store
___D. I don't know.

12. Why do we have rules?
___A. Because our parents and teachers say so.
___B. Because mean people made them.
___C. To help us resolve disagreements between people.
___D. I don't know.

13. What is an election?
___A. When people vote to choose a winner.
___B. A game played by adults.
___C. Something on TV.
___D. I don't know.

14. What is culture?
___A. Sharing your favorite food.
___B. Wearing fancy clothes to a restaurant.
___C. The traditions and way of life of a particular group of people.
___D. I don't know

```
┌─────────────────────────────────────┐
│  MAP LANDFORM OPTIONS                 │
│  beach          ocean                 │
│  cave           plain                 │
│  desert         pond                  │
│  forest         river                 │
│  hill           swamp                 │
│  iceberg        valley                │
│  island         volcano               │
│  lake           waterfall             │
│  mountain                             │
└─────────────────────────────────────┘
```

COMMUNITY ROLE OPTIONS
bold = essential
others = optional once essentials claimed

FOOD & WATER
farmer
fisherman
grocery store
restaurant
water treatment plant

SHELTER
construction company
building materials store

CLOTHING
cotton farm
cloth & clothing factory
clothing store
shoemaker
shoe store

EDUCATION & SERVICE
school
library
church/mosque/temple
community center
college
book store
museum

CLEAN UP
trash and recycling company
car wash
Laundromat

GOVERNMENT & SAFETY
fire station
police station
post office
city hall

HEALTH
medical clinic
hospital

TRANSPORTATION
bus company
trucking company
car dealership
bike shop
train station

UTILITIES
electric & gas company
solar and wind power company
telephone & internet company

RECREATION
park and playground
fitness center
toy store
movie theater
zoo

MISC.
beauty shop
boat builder
etc.

LIFE IN PUPPETLAND

My Name _____

My job is _____

I help provide one of the basic human needs: _ yes _ no

I sell: ___ Goods: _____ ___ Services: _____
                    (what)   (what)
Who pays me for my goods or services? ___ consumers ___ the government

When I need _____for my business, I go to _____
                                                      (other business)
And when I need _____for my business, I go to _____
                                                           (other business)
I like my job because _____

For fun, I go to _____ in my town.
                        (other business)
My favorite natural landform in Puppet Land is _____

My favorite man made place in Puppet Land is _____

- -

LIFE IN PUPPETLAND

My Name _____

My job is _____

I help provide one of the basic human needs: _ yes _ no

I sell: ___ Goods: _____ ___ Services: _____
                    (what)   (what)
Who pays me for my goods or services? ___ consumers ___ the government

When I need _____for my business, I go to _____
                                                      (other business)
And when I need _____for my business, I go to _____
                                                           (other business)
I like my job because _____

For fun, I go to _____ in my town.
                        (other business)
My favorite natural landform in Puppet Land is _____

My favorite man made place in Puppet Land is _____

84

Name _____ Date _____

How Did I Do?
PUPPET CITY

AS A THINKER
1. I thought about how my puppet's job connected to the rest of the community.

    *   ***   *****

AS AN ART MAKER

2. I created a map with five natural landforms.

    *   ***   *****

3. I designed my building for the business I was responsible for.

    *   ***   *****

4. I completed my puppet.

    *   ***   *****

AS A PERFORMER

5. I used my puppet as requested for its role in the community.

    *   ***   *****

6. I took dramatic play time seriously and did my best to bring our community to life.

    *   ***   *****

7. I listened to my class members' puppets in our different tasks, such as trading goods and services.

    *   ***   *****

_____

8. My thoughts on the experience (use back of paper if needed):

PROJECT TEN: US AND THEM
Driving Question: How is point of view connected to understanding history?

Grades: 3 - 5

Overview
Students research and build puppets for performances demonstrating the significance of point of view in historical documentation.
Time: Three or more 45 minute class sessions, depending on puppet technique selected (excluding research).

ORGANIZE AND PREPARE

1. **SELECT** a puppet technique and gather materials.
QUICKEST: Hand Puppets: Recycled Bottle Head (p.139)
LONGER: Miming Puppet: Recycled Bottle Head (p.149)
2. **DIVIDE** class in working pairs.
3. **PRINT**
• **ONE SET** of Viewpoint Worksheets for each pair of students (p.88, 89, 90)
• ONE Viewpoint Project Planning Sheet/pair (p.91)
• ONE Viewpoint Project Checklist/pair (p.92)
• Project Self Evaluation – one/student (p.93)
• Teamwork & Focus Rubric - one/student (p.170)

CORE STANDARDS:
SOCIAL STUDIES:
History: Historical Thinking Skills; Historical People, Events, and Symbols
LANGUAGE ARTS:
Reading for Informational Text: Key Ideas and Details; Integration of Knowledge and Ideas
Speaking and Listening: Comprehension and Collaboration; Presentation of Knowledge and Ideas

EXPECTED LEARNING OUTCOMES:
Students will be able to analyze facts in order to differentiate between points of view in a historical event.
Students will be able to compose a dramatic production to present researched facts.
Students will be able to evaluate the effectiveness of dramatic presentations.

INTRODUCE

History is the study of the stories of events that happened in the past. Many of these stories are about conflicts or disagreements. So, the story you would hear about the event may depend on who is telling it. You are going to work with a partner to bring to life two historical figures who had different viewpoints about a particular event in history. Examples could be European explorers in America vs. Native Americans or present day conservationists vs. the oil industry. You will research both sides of the issue, then each make a puppet to present their viewpoints to each other and to the class. Every group will receive a Project Check List. We will read it together now. (Read aloud) So, you see that this includes all the steps needed to complete the project as well as tips to effectively use your puppets.
Each group will choose a Check List Manager. Their job is to check off each step as it is finished. When it is time to rehearse your story, you may ask a member of another group to be your director. The Director will look at the Performance Elements and watch your show to help and advise you on using those well.

VOCABULARY:
viewpoint: a way of looking at or thinking about something
truth: the real facts

FOCUS

1. Assign students specific events to research which would be seen differently, depending on who is telling the story.
2. Groups select a Checklist Manager to keep track of tasks and goals on Checklist for selected technique.
3. Pairs complete Viewpoint Worksheets, researching events and people as needed.

CREATE

Make puppets and props.

REHEARSE

Partners work together to plan the presentation:

• as a debate

• as an interview: A student or puppet may serve as host of the interview talk show entitled, "What's the Problem?" on which the puppets are both guests.

• A student or puppet serve as judge in a courtroom drama in which one of the puppets is accusing the other of wrongdoing. Each must state the facts of their case and the judge will make a decision. The decision may or may not be what actually happened in history.

NOTE: Students should be able to improvise their dialogue, based on the research already done.

* Students perform work for the class, with class Constructive Critique (p.171).

SHARE

Schedule a performance:

• for younger classes

• for classes doing the same project, to compare and contrast results

• for parents at an open house or other event

• encourage visiting audiences to write comments with their thoughts after the debates or mock court cases to submit to the performers

TIP: Small audiences are best so that puppeteers' voices may be heard, unless amplification is available that does not necessitate leaning in to a microphone.

REFLECT

What does viewpoint have to do with the study of history? Are news reports in newspapers, magazines, on television or online necessarily the truth? How can you find out?

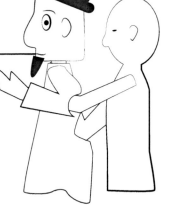

ASSESS

Teacher: Performance based as well as Teamwork & Focus Rubric (p.172)
Student: Self Evaluation: Viewpoint (p.93)

Partner Names:

Viewpoint # 1_____

Viewpoint # 2_____

Fill out this page with your partner. Then fill out one of the other pages for your character alone, researching as needed to get facts.

What is the focus event or issue?

Why is this event or issue controversial (causing disagreement)?

Who are the people involved?

The problem is caused by:

Viewpoint # 1:

Viewpoint # 2:

Was one viewpoint held by a majority of people at that time?

Has that changed in the present time?

Your name _____

Viewpoint # 1 Worksheet

Viewpoint # 1 Character (person from history) Name: _____

When does this event take place?

Where does this event take place?

Who else is involved?

What does your character think about this?

Why?

What is at stake (What would your character lose)?

Story details in sequential order:

Your name _____

Viewpoint # 2 Worksheet

Viewpoint # 1 Character (person from history) Name: _____

When does this event take place?

Where does this event take place?

Who else is involved?

What does your character think about this?

Why?

What is at stake (What would your character lose)?

Story details in sequential order:

VIEWPOINT PRESENTATION PLANNING SHEET

Your presentation must clearly show at least two opposing viewpoints around an actual event in history. The audience should be able to understand the facts and significant events. You may use props as needed (maps, documents, photos) as well as additional characters as first person witnesses for either side.
Complete this sheet as a short plan. You will NOT use this during performance, but instead will improvise the dialogue based on your research.

PRESENTATION FORMAT:
___ Debate
___ Interview
___ Court case
___ Other _____

CHARACTERS:

SETTING (Location and date):

The BEGINNING should answer the following questions:
Who are the main characters? Do these characters represent a larger group? When and where does the event take place? What do the main characters want?

The MIDDLE is the main conflict of the presentation.
What problem(s) keeps the main characters from getting what they want?

The END resolves the conflict.
How do the characters succeed, or fail, at resolving the issue? How is justice involved? If this happened long ago, does this problem remain today?

VIEWPOINT PROJECT CHECKLIST AND MIMING PUPPET PERFORMANCE CRITERIA

GROUP MEMBERS: _____

_____

PREPARATION: OUR GROUP (check as each part is completed)
worked together to plan the presentation by:
___ a. doing enough research from several sources to be familiar with our assigned characters.
___ d. completing the Viewpoint Worksheets.
___ b. listening to our partners' ideas.
___ c. sharing our own ideas.
___ d. in planning our presentation, writing a plan, NOT a complete script as a debate,
interview or other format
___ built the puppets as instructed.
___ made sure our puppets had noses that form a strong side view profile shape
___ selected very lightweight puppet clothing material
___ finished all puppets and props required for the story.
___ used the tools properly and put them away when finished.
___ did not waste materials.
___ practiced the presentation.

PERFORMANCE ELEMENTS FOR CRITIQUE
Use the following for rehearsal goals, and for basis of Constructive Critique after the performance.
___ The presentation is written around the assigned topic.
___ The presentation format is clear and shows issues around the two viewpoints
___ The puppets are held so that the audience sees their bodies, above the bottom edge of clothing
___ The puppets face the audience, "cheating out" to face each other at an angle in conversation
___ Puppets make conversations clear by moving when talking, using hand gesture
___ The puppets' movements have purpose: to show action and emotion.
___ If no back curtain, puppeteers DO NOT make eye contact with audience, but remain
strongly focused on their puppet.
___ Loud, clear, un-rushed voices allow the audience to hear.
___ The group does not bring script or notes to the stage.
___ As performers or audience, group members are polite and respectful at all times.

Name _____ Date _____

How Did I Do?
VIEWPOINT AND HISTORY

AS A RESEARCHER AND WRITER
1. I worked with my partner to learn facts about our historical figures.

    *   ***   *****

2. I worked with my partner to complete the Viewpoint Worksheets.

    *   ***   *****

3. I worked with my partner to plan our presentation.

    *   ***   *****

AS AN ART MAKER
4. I completed the puppet of my historical figure.

    *   ***   *****

AS A PERFORMER
5. I cooperated with my partner to present the work we had created.

    *   ***   *****

6. I did not take any script on stage, but improvised the script based on our research,

    *   ***   *****

7. I took the performance seriously and did my best to bring my character to life.

    *   ***   *****

8. I listened to the critique.

    *   ***   *****

AS AN AUDIENCE MEMBER
9. I watched the shows quietly.

    *   ***   *****

10. I gave polite and thoughtful comments in critique.

    *   ***   *****

_____

11. My thoughts on the experience (use back of paper if needed):

PROJECT ELEVEN: CULTURE AND MYTH
Driving Question: What is the connection between myths and culture?

Grades: 3 – 5

Overview
Students analyze a myth of a particular culture and create puppets to perform it.
Time: Four or more 45 minute class sessions, depending on puppet technique selected.

ORGANIZE AND PREPARE

1. Select several short myths from the culture being studied.
2. Select a puppet technique and gather materials.
QUICKEST: Shadow Puppets (p.155)
Shadow puppets are potentially quicker, although a shadow production can be quite complex and refined, depending on time available. Shadow puppets can accommodate a large number of characters (encourage students to leave out non-essential characters – determine importance!) Shadows are also good for scenes of flying, underwater, etc.
LONGER: Hand Puppets: Recycled Bottle Head (p.139), Newspaper and masking tape head (p.140), Toy Theater (p.162)
3. **PRINT**
• Story Planning Sheet: one/group (p.96)
• Puppet Project Checklist for selected puppetry technique - one per group (Section IV)
• Project Self Evaluation – one/student (p.97)
• Teamwork & Focus Rubric - one/student (p.170)

CORE STANDARDS: SOCIAL STUDIES:
History: Historical Thinking Skills;
Historical People, Events, and Symbols
LANGUAGE ARTS:
Reading for Informational Text: Key Ideas and Details; Integration of Knowledge and Ideas
Speaking and Listening: Comprehesion and Collaboration; Presentation of Knowledge and Ideas

EXPECTED LEARNING OUTCOMES:
Students will be able to analyze a myth for its connection to the beliefs of a culture
Students will be able to dramatize a myth using puppets.
Students will be able to evaluate their own and others work based on specific goals and standards.

INTRODUCE

VOCABULARY:
myth: a story that was told in an ancient culture to explain a practice, belief, or natural occurrence
culture: the traditions and way of life of a particular group of people
supernatural: not able to be explained by the laws of nature, as magic

The word "myth" comes from Greece, meaning "to tell a story". Since ancient times, people in every culture have told stories to explain the mysteries of the world around them. A myth is not based on fact and often involves characters with supernatural powers. Myths carry a message sometimes about how life began or explain a natural event. Myths are often believed to be true by the people whose culture they are from and may be the basis of beliefs and religions. Myths contain wisdom that is shared and unifying to a culture. You will work in groups to bring

94

myths to life with puppets.

Every group will receive a Project Check List. We will read it together now. (Read aloud) So, you see that this includes all the steps needed to complete the project as well as tips to effectively use your puppets.

Each group will choose a Check List Manager. Their job is to check off each step as it is finished. When it is time to rehearse your story, you may ask a member of another group to be your director. The Director will look at the Performance Elements and watch your show to help and advise you on using those well.

FOCUS

1. Assign students specific myths from the culture being studied, so that each group of 4 – 5 work on a different myth.
2. Groups select a Checklist Manager to keep track of tasks and goals on Checklist for selected technique.
3. Groups complete Story Planning Sheet: Mythology to clarify story, researching events and appearance of characters as needed.

CREATE

Make puppets and props.

REHEARSE

1. Students organize puppets and props and practice with their group.
For further performance ideas, see Performance Considerations Sheet.
2. Students perform work for the class, with class Constructive Critique (p.171).

SHARE

Schedule a performance:
• for younger classes
• for classes doing the same project, to compare and contrast results
• for parents at an open house or other event
• if several classes participate, hold a Culture Celebration: an evening event with scheduled shows in different classrooms, perhaps with food and other displays from that culture.
TIP: Small audiences are best so that puppeteers' voices may be heard, unless amplification is available that does not necessitate leaning in to a microphone.

REFLECT

What can we learn about a culture from their myths? What similarities and differences do you see in comparing myths of other cultures to familiar stories from your own culture?

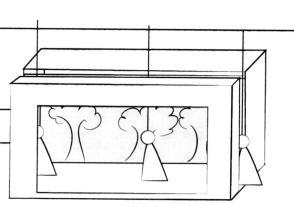

ASSESS

Teacher: Performance based as well as Teamwork & Focus Rubric (p.170)
Student: Self Evaluation: Mythology (p.97)

Group Members' Names:

OUR MYTH TITLE:

FROM WHAT CULTURE:

DOES THE MYTH EXPLAIN A BEGINNING OR A NATURAL EVENT? IF SO, WHAT?

DOES THE MYTH INVOLVE THE SUPERNATURAL IN ANY WAY? HOW?

WHAT MESSAGE DOES THIS MYTH COMMUNICATE?

OUR STORY SETTING: (Where does the story take place?)
Include short description of setting(s)

OUR STORY CHARACTERS: (Who is in the story?)
Include short description of who characters are and their relationships to each other

OUR STORY PLOT: (What happens in the story?)
1. BEGINNING (Should show who and where are the characters and what are their relationships):

2. MIDDLE (What problem develops for the characters to solve?):

3. END (How do the characters solve the problem?):

WORK PLAN: (List of who will construct each puppet and prop for your story) Use back as needed.
NAME: JOB:

Name _____ Date _____

How Did I Do?
MYTHOLOGY

AS A WRITER
1. I worked with my team to understand our assigned myth.

     *   ***   *****

2. I worked with my team to complete the Story Planning Sheet.

     *   ***   *****

3. I worked with my team to plan our presentation.

     *   ***   *****

AS AN ART MAKER
4. I completed the puppet(s) that were my responsibility for our story.

     *   ***   *****

AS A PERFORMER
5. I cooperated with my team to present the work we had created.

     *   ***   *****

6. I did not take any script on stage, but improvised the script based on our research,

     *   ***   *****

7. I took the performance seriously and did my best to bring my character to life.

     *   ***   *****

8. I listened to the critique.

     *   ***   *****

AS AN AUDIENCE MEMBER
9. I watched the shows quietly.

     *   ***   *****

10. I gave polite and thoughtful comments in critique.

     *   ***   *****

_____

11. My thoughts on the experience (use back of paper if needed):

PROJECT TWELVE: CYCLES OF CHANGE
Driving Question: What do different life cycles have in common?

Grades: K – 2

Overview
Students analyze life cycles of living organisms as well as natural and man made cycles then create simple puppets to perform the cycles in sequence. Featured cycles are of bird, butterfly, plant, frog, water, and plastic.
Time: one-two 45 minute classes

CORE STANDARDS: LANGUAGE ARTS
Reading for Informational Text: Key Ideas and Details; Integration of Knowledge and Ideas Speaking and Listening: Comprehension and Collaboration; Presentation of Knowledge and Ideas

ORGANIZE AND PREPARE
1. PRINT
- Life Cycle Sequence Drawings (p.100-105)
- Shadow Puppet Project Checklist (p.168) one/group
- Project Self Evaluation – one/student (p.106)
- Teamwork & Focus Rubric - one/student (p.170)
2. GATHER materials for suggested puppet technique:
Shadow Puppets: Assembled Shape (p.156)
3. Additional Materials:
colored markers or crayons

EXPECTED LEARNING OUTCOMES:
Students will be able to place in order elements of life cycles in nature.
Students will be able to create a puppet to represent a specific natural element.
Students will be able to compare similarities and differences in various natural cycles.

INTRODUCE
All living things and some non-living things go through changes over time, called cycles. You are going to decorate some cycles to learn the correct order, then make puppets to bring these cycles to life.

FOCUS
Divide students in groups of four. Each group receives a Life Cycle page for the same cycle. Each student uses crayon or marker to trace around the shapes in the steps of the cycle.

CREATE

VOCABULARY:
life cycle: sequence of changes undergone by an organism during its life
metamorphosis: a major change in some animals or insects that happens as the animal becomes an adult
ALSO: words on Cycle Choices sheet Page

Observing the shapes, students recreate these using pre-cut geometric shaped of black paper, glued or stapled together, punching holes as needed. Complete shadow puppets with a bendable straw control rod.

REHEARSE
Students work in groups, each with a single puppet, to perform their cycle in sequence on the shadow screen.
TIP: The illusion of one puppet becoming another can be done as follows:

1. Hold first puppet firmly against shadow screen, making sure to grasp rod as far away as possible from puppet.

2. SLOWLY pull the puppet straight back from screen (NOT up or down – just lift back, away from screen) so shadow gradually disappears.

3. Move next puppet SLOWLY to screen to exactly the same spot the first puppet just left.

4. Hold firmly against screen and move as needed.

• Add narration, possibly with music or sound effects for each cycle presentation. (See Sound Effects Orchestra p.172).

SHARE

Schedule a performance:
• for younger classes
• for classes doing the same project, to compare and contrast results
• for parents at an open house or other event
• as part of a science or ecology festival

REFLECT

What similarities did you see in the life cycle of the frog and the butterfly? What was different? What is a part of the water cycle you have seen in real life? What would you predict happened after what you described? Why is plastic recycling a good idea?

ASSESS

Teacher: Performance based as well as Teamwork & Focus Rubric (p.170)
Student: Self Evaluation: Cycles of Change (p.106)

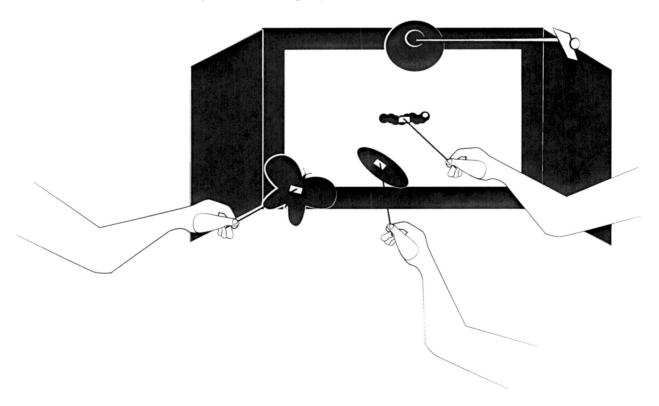

BIRD Life Cycle

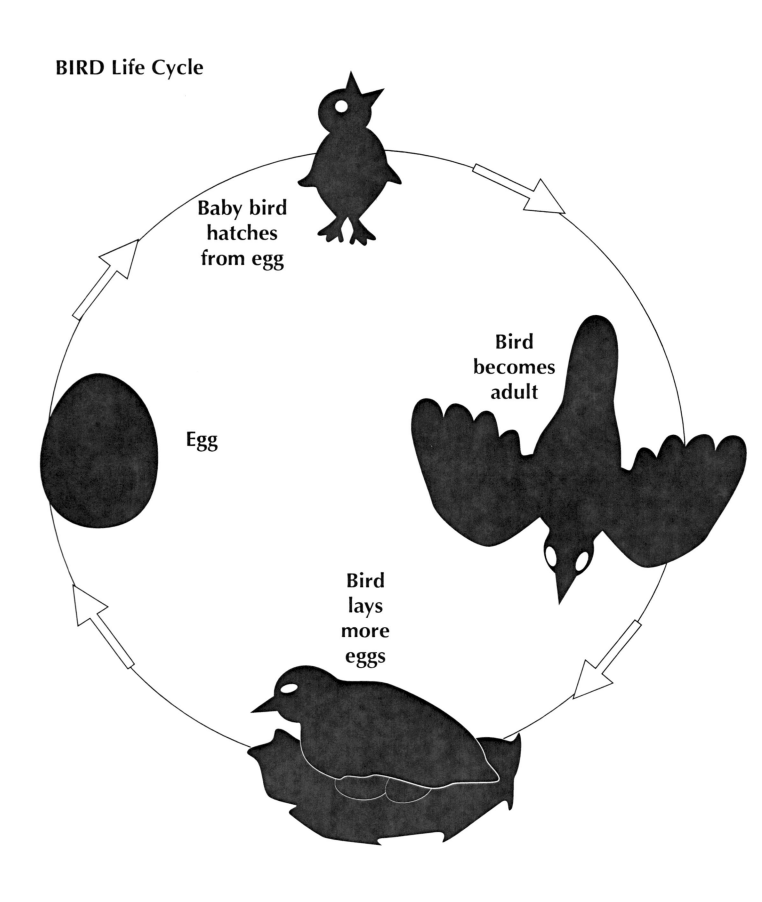

Baby bird
hatches
from egg

Egg

Bird
becomes
adult

Bird
lays
more
eggs

BUTTERFLY Life Cycle

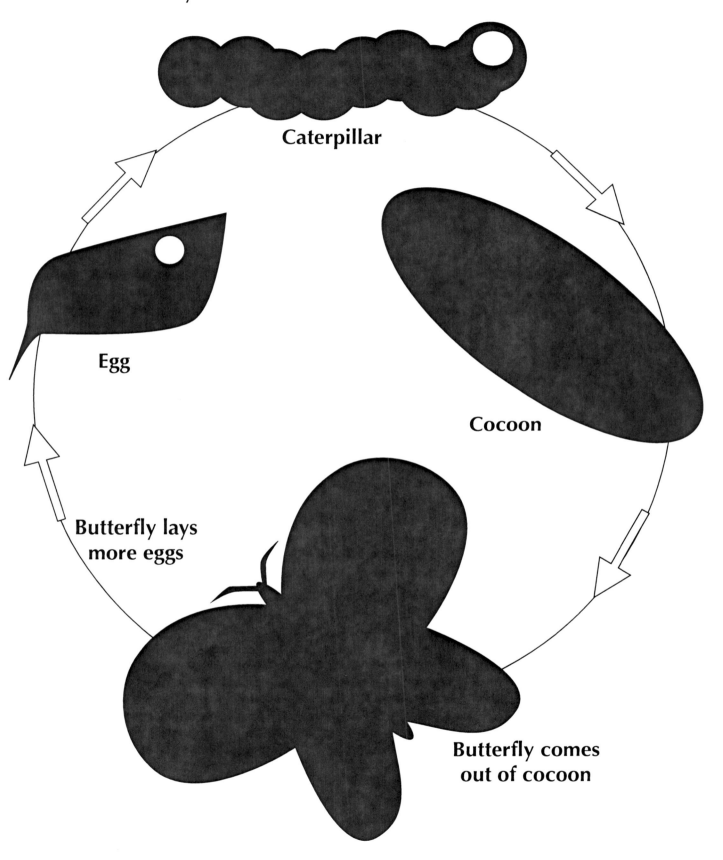

Caterpillar

Egg

Cocoon

Butterfly lays more eggs

Butterfly comes out of cocoon

FROG Life Cycle

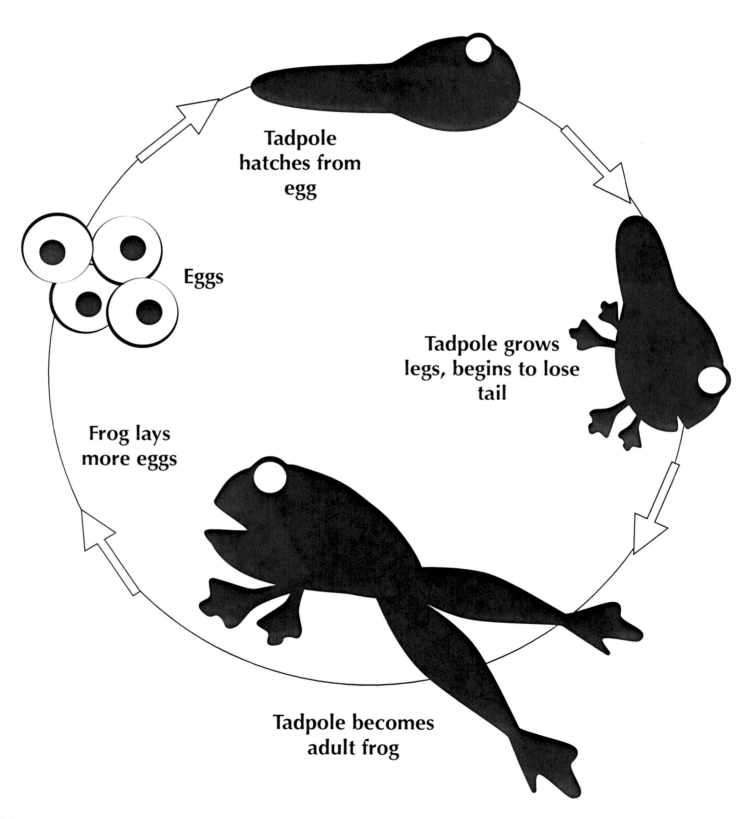

Tadpole
hatches from
egg

Eggs

Tadpole grows
legs, begins to lose
tail

Frog lays
more eggs

Tadpole becomes
adult frog

PLANT Life Cycle

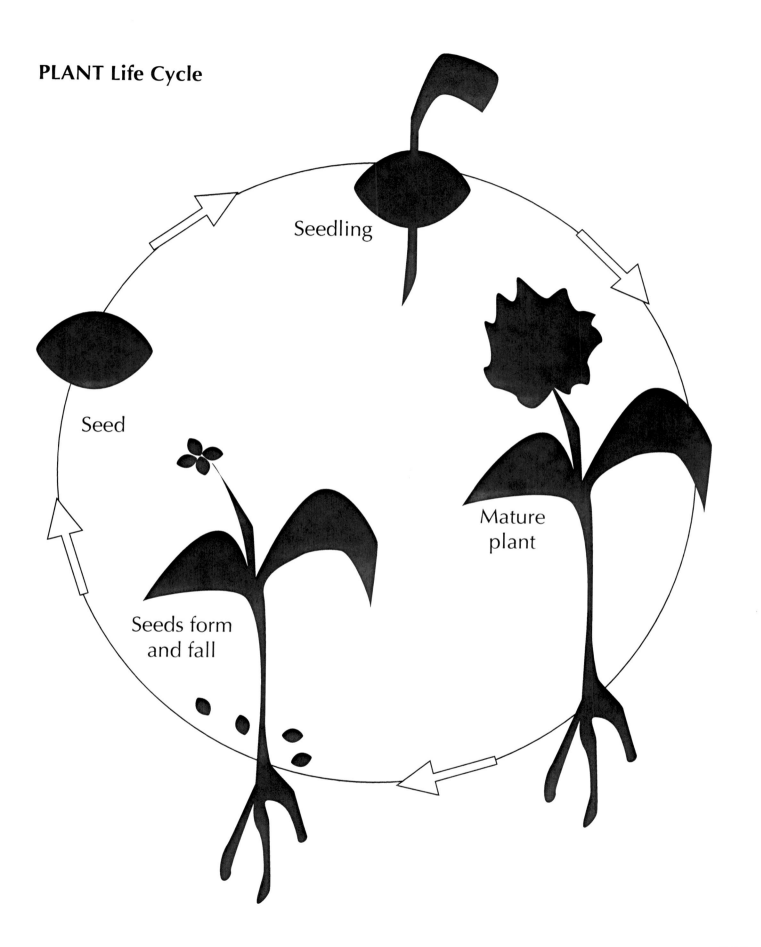

Seedling

Seed

Mature plant

Seeds form and fall

WATER Cycle

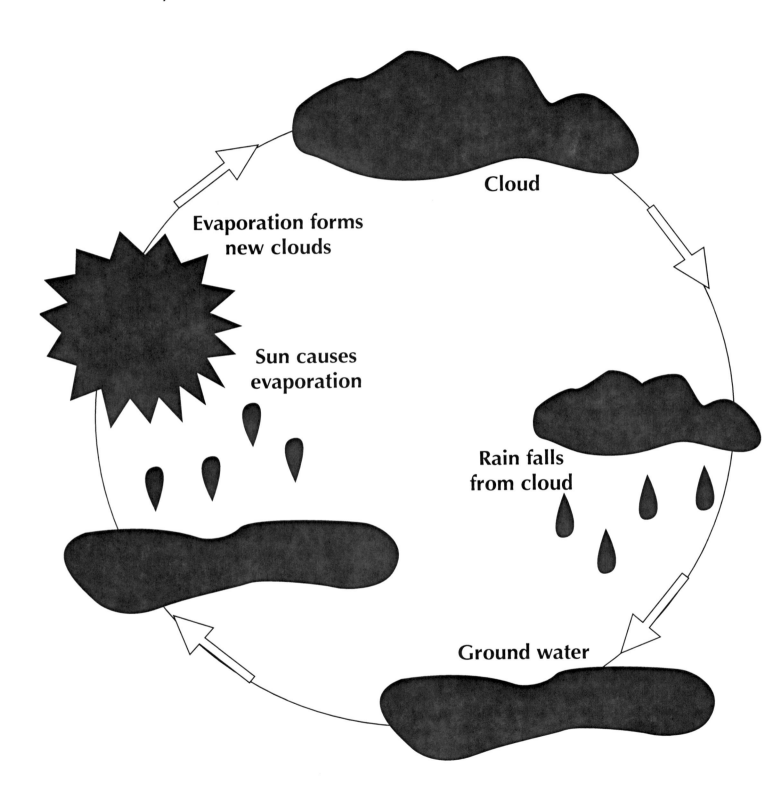

Cloud

Evaporation forms
new clouds

Sun causes
evaporation

Rain falls
from cloud

Ground water

PLASTIC Recycling

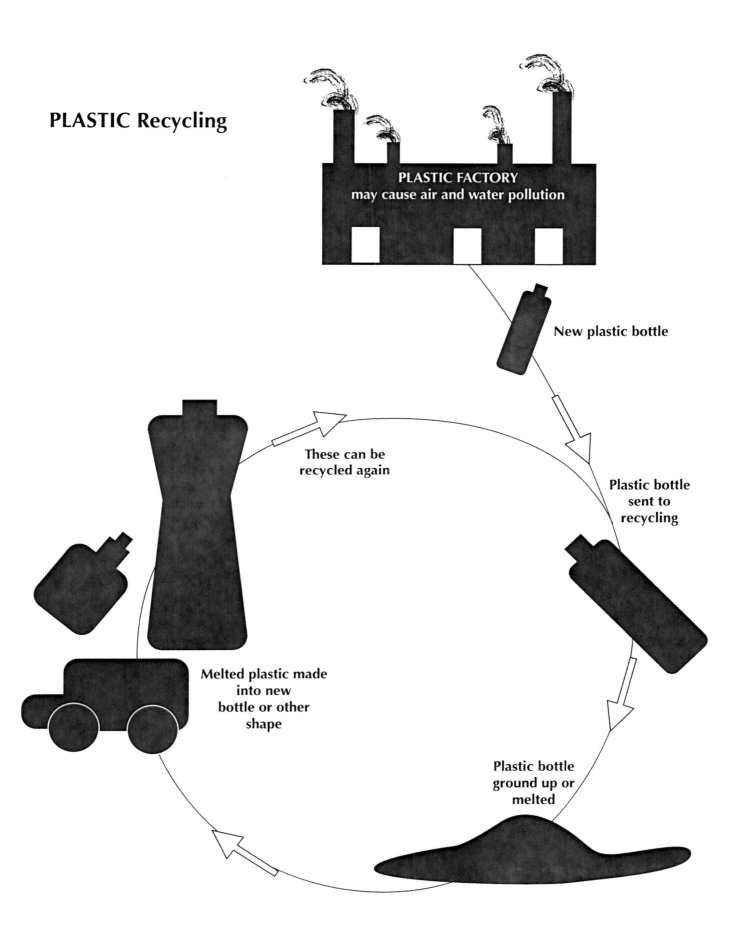

PLASTIC FACTORY
may cause air and water pollution

New plastic bottle

These can be
recycled again

Plastic bottle
sent to
recycling

Melted plastic made
into new
bottle or other
shape

Plastic bottle
ground up or
melted

Name _____ Date _____

How Did I Do?
CYCLES IN SCIENCE

Circle the number of stars that you think best describe your work for each question.

AS A THINKER
1. I understood that each step in the life cycle must go in the correct sequence.

      *   ***   *****

AS AN ART MAKER
2. I made a puppet for the part of the life cycle I was assigned.

      *   ***   *****

AS A PERFORMER:
3. I cooperated with my group to use my puppet to show my part of the cycle.

      *   ***   *****

4. I operated my puppet so that the audience could see it.

      *   ***   *****

AS AN AUDIENCE MEMBER:
5. I watched each performance quietly.

      *   ***   *****

6. I was polite and thoughtful in my performance reaction comments.

      *   ***   *****

_____

7. My thoughts on the experience (use back of paper if needed):

Name _____ Date _____

How Did I Do?
ANIMALS AND ECOLOGY

AS A RESEARCHER AND WRITER
1. I worked to learn facts about the assigned animal and completed the Animal Study Page.

     *   ***   *****

2. I worked with my partners to complete the Story Planning – Fact Connect Page.

     *   ***   *****

3. I worked with my partners to plan our presentation.

     *   ***   *****

AS AN ART MAKER
4. I helped complete the scenery and puppets for our habitat.

     *   ***   *****

AS A PERFORMER
5. I cooperated with my partners to present the work we had created.

     *   ***   *****

6. I did not take any script on stage, but improvised the script based on our research.

     *   ***   *****

7. I took the performance seriously and did my best to bring my character to life.

     *   ***   *****

8. I listened to the critique.

     *   ***   *****

AS AN AUDIENCE MEMBER
9. I watched the shows quietly.

     *   ***   *****

10. I gave polite and thoughtful comments in critique.

     *   ***   *****

_____

11. My thoughts on the experience (use back of paper if needed):

PROJECT THIRTEEN: HAPPY HABITAT
Driving Question: How do the wild animals you see find what they need to survive?

Grades: 3 – 5

Overview
Students collaborate to research local animal habits and habitats then create a realistic story to dramatize a day in the life of the animal using Toy Theater puppet technique.
Time: Three - four 45 minute class sessions

CORE STANDARDS: LANGUAGE ARTS
Reading for Informational Text: Key Ideas and Details; Integration of Knowledge and Ideas
Speaking and Listening: Comprehension and Collaboration; Presentation of Knowledge and Ideas

ORGANIZE AND PREPARE

1. **GATHER** materials for recommended puppet technique: Toy Theater (p.162)
2. **PRINT**
• Animal Habitat Study Pages – one/student (p.110)
• Story Planning: Facts Connect Page – one/group (p.111)
• Project Checklist for selected Puppetry Technique (Section IV)
• Project Self Evaluation – one/student (p.107)
• Teamwork & Focus Rubric - one/student (p.170)

EXPECTED LEARNING OUTCOMES:
Students will be able to analyze and connect animal adaptation to habitat.
Students will be able to compose a dramatic sequence to inform an audience of specific facts.
Students will be able to evaluate student work for success in delineated goals.

VOCABULARY:

ecology: the relationship between a group of living things and their environment

ecosystem: a community of plants and animals that depend on each other for survival

adaptation: a change in a plant or animal making it better suited to survive in a particular place

habitat: the place an animal finds basic needs, which include food, water, air, and shelter

preservation: to keep something in good condition, safe from harm or loss

INTRODUCE

Animals need to live in a habitat where they can find what they need for survival: food, water, air, and shelter. Animals may change, or adapt, in order to survive if their habitat changes for any reason.
You are going to work with partners to research a wild animal that you have seen near where you live. You will learn about how it is adapted to the habitat where it lives. You will examine how people are helpful, or a problem, for its survival, as well as whether the animal is helpful or a problem for people. Then, you will create a realistic story of a day in the animal's life including facts about the animal, as well as how it is adapted to this habitat. Your group will then use puppet theater to present what you learned in a story format.
Every group will receive a Project Check List. We will read it together now. (Read aloud) So, you see that this includes all the steps needed to complete the project as well as tips

to effectively use your puppets.

Each group will choose a Check List Manager. Their job is to check off each step as it is finished. When it is time to rehearse your story, you may ask a member of another group to be your director. The Director will look at the Performance Elements and watch your show to help and advise you on using those well.

FOCUS
1. Students are grouped in twos or threes.
2. Groups are assigned or select an animal to research.
3. Groups select a Checklist Manager to keep track of tasks and goals on Toy Theater Checklist.
4. Students research and complete Animal Habitat sheet.
5. Students complete Story Planning: Facts Connect sheet.

NOTE ON PRESENTATION STYLE: Students may choose to have their animals speak, but, other than that, the characters must remain in their realistic world

CREATE
1. Students construct toy theater habitats, using paper and natural materials.
2. Students construct puppets.

REHEARSE
1. Students practice their fact based stories, demonstrating a beginning, middle, and end.
2. Students perform work for the class, with class Constructive Critique (p.171).

SHARE
Schedule a performance:
• for younger classes
• for classes doing the same project, to compare and contrast results
• for parents at an open house or other event
• Host an "Animals Around Us" event to invite community members to share and learn about beneficial and problem local animals. Invite speakers from the local SPCA, pest control, bird watching society, etc.

TIP: Small audiences are best so that puppeteers' voices may be heard, unless amplification is available that does not necessitate leaning in to a microphone.

REFLECT
Describe your experience creating a story using factual material. What facts did you learn from some of the presentations? How will you think differently about animals around us?

ASSESS
Teacher: Performance based as well as Teamwork & Focus Rubric (p.170)
Student Self Evaluation: Habitats (p.107)

Animal Habitat Study

Name _____

Animal _____

Habitat _____

Natural elements of habitat:

Man-made elements of habitat:

Food found in habitat:

Water found in habitat:

Shelter found in habitat:

Shelter for young found in habitat:

How is protection from predators connected to habitat?

How is animal's life cycle adapted to habitat?

What other animals live in habitat? What is their relationship to focus animal?
(Prey, predator, one helpful to the other, or the opposite, or none)

Are people helpful or a problem for this animal's survival?

What should be done?

Is this animal helpful or a problem to people?

What should be done?

Group Members' Names:

TITLE: A Day in the Life of a _____ in _____
                                           (animal)   (street or neighborhood name)

SETTING: (Where does the story take place?)

CHARACTERS: (Who is in the story?)

FACTS DEMONSTRATED IN OUR PRESENTATION:
1. About the animal:

2. About the animal's adaptation to its habitat:

3. About human dangers to the animal's survival, and/or problem animal causes for humans:

PLOT: (What happens in the story?)
1. BEGINNING (Who and where are the characters and what are their relationships?):

2. MIDDLE (What problem develops for the main character to solve?):

3. END (How does the character solve the problem?):

WORK PLAN: (List of who will construct each puppet and prop. Use back if needed.)
NAME: JOB:

LESSON FOURTEEN: STORY IN ART
Driving Question: How can you see a painting as part of a story?

Grades: K - 2, 3 - 5

Overview
Students use Visual Thinking Strategies to analyze a work of art, then create stories inspired by the imagery, brought to life with puppets.
Time: One-two (Grades 1-2) or three-four (Grades 3-5) 45 minute class sessions

Grades First through Second create storyboards of a familiar tale, then make puppets to collaborate in a presentation of the story in sequetial scenes.

Grades Three through Five collaborate in specific roles to write a simple story, make puppets, and perform their work.

ORGANIZE AND PREPARE: GRADES K - 2

1. **SELECT** a work of art.
Realistic or semi-abstract work by well-known artists, featuring imagery suggesting at least two people and/or animals involved in action and/or emotion are effective to inspire thought on story.

EXPECTED LEARNING OUTCOMES:
Students will be able to describe specific elements in a work of art.
Students will be able to interpret their observations to create related art.
Students will be able to evaluate connections between the student art and the paintings.

VOCABULARY:
image: a picture, or the thought of how something looks or might look

visual: related to seeing or the eyes

abstract: expressing ideas and emotions in art through elements like colors and lines, without necessarily trying to create a realistic image

realistic: in art, showing things as they are in real life

shape: the form or outline of something

2. **SELECT** a puppet technique and gather materials.
QUICKEST: Rod Puppets: Assembled Shape (p.147)
LONGER: Rod Puppets: Flat Head Two Rod Puppets – or any technique that reflects the art selected, possibly incorporating recycled materials (p.154)
3. **PRINT**:
• Project Self Evaluation – one/student (p.117)
• Teamwork & Focus Rubric - one/student (p.170)

INTRODUCE
This is a painting called _____ by the famous artist _____ . We are going to study this painting and then imagine what might have happened just before or just after what the artist painted. Then you will make puppets to show everyone your ideas.

FOCUS

1. Observe and discuss work of art using the Visual Thinking Strategies (http://www.vt-shome.org/) format:

What is going on in this picture?

What do you see that makes you say that?

What else can we find?

REPEAT above questions for each student until all have made comments.

If this were just one picture painted to tell a whole story, and what we see are the characters the story is about, what do you think they might have been doing just before this painting was made? What about just after?

You will start by making puppets of these characters. Try to make your puppets so they look like they belong in the painting, so think about what colors the artist used. What kind of shapes? Are there people? Animals? Plants or other things you recognize?

CREATE

1. Make puppets.

REHEARSE

Perform brief scenes for class, improvising words as needed. Student should say if this is a Before or After scene.

Highlight the differences in different students' ideas.

SHARE

Schedule a sharing session:

- for younger classes
- for classes doing the same project, to compare and contrast results
- for parents at an open house or other event
- Students may further elaborate their stories by writing them down in storyboard format.

REFLECT

What story ideas did other students image that you had not thought of? What do you think the artist would think of your ideas?

ASSESS

Teacher: Performance based
Student Self Evaluation: Story In Art K-2 (p.117)

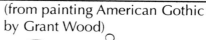
(from painting American Gothic by Grant Wood)

ORGANIZE AND PREPARE: GRADES 3 - 5

1. **SELECT** a sample work of art to analyze as a class. *Realistic or semi-abstract work by well-known artists, featuring imagery suggesting at least two people and/or animals involved in action and/or emotion are effective to inspire thought on story.*

2. **SELECT** a variety of works of art from which students may choose. Ideally, postcard sized prints are made available, for students to refer to frequently in development of the work.

3. **GATHER** materials for Puppet Technique: Toy Theater is ideal for this project.

4. **PRINT**
   - Check List – Toy Theater – one/group (p.169)
   - Story Planning Sheet – one/group (p.116)
   - Project Self Evaluation – one/student (p.117)
   - Teamwork & Focus Rubric - one/student (p.170)

INTRODUCE

You are beginning a project in which you will create a story inspired by a work of art. First, we will look at a painting and see what we can do to understand what it is about.

We will use Visual Thinking Strategies by answering three simple questions to go deeper into the painting's meaning. Using this strategy will help you analyze the image you work with to find inspiration for a story.

What is going on in this picture?

What do you see that makes you say that?

What else can we find?

REPEAT above questions for each student until all have made comments.

Further information: http://www.vtshome.org/

FOCUS

Now, student groups of 2 – 4 people will select a work of art to inspire a story. The story does not have to use words, but it does have to show a beginning, middle, and end. You might want to add music and/or sound effects later. You will start by completing your group's Story Planning Sheet. Then, you will use Toy Theater puppetry to bring your story to life: You will use a cardboard box as your stage. Decorate your box by adding scenery. The scenery should reflect the colors and shapes of your selected painting. Then, you will make paper puppets as the characters in your story. Anything can be brought to life as a puppet, so your puppets do not have to be people or animals – they may be shapes you see as coming to life for your story.

Every group will receive a Project Check List. We will read it together now.

So, you see that this includes all the steps needed to complete the project as well as tips to effectively use your puppets.

Each group will choose a Check List Manager. Their job is to check off each step as it is finished. When it is time to rehearse your story, you may ask a member of another group to be your director. The Director will look at the Performance Elements and watch your show to help and advise you on using those well.

CREATE

1. Groups select a Checklist Manager to keep track of tasks and goals on Checklist for selected technique.
2. Groups complete Story Development Sheets to clarify story.
3. Make puppets and scenery (in each group's own box stage)

REHEARSE

1. Students organize puppets and props and practice with their group.
2. Students perform work for the class, with class Constructive Critique (p.171).

SHARE

Schedule a performance:
• for younger classes
• for classes doing the same project, to compare and contrast results
• for parents at an open house or other event
• as part of a school wide art show
TIP: Small audiences are best so that puppeteers' voices may be heard, unless amplification is available that does not necessitate leaning in to a microphone.

REFLECT

Which elements of your selected art work most inspired your story? Why?

ASSESS

Teacher: Performance based as well as Teamwork & Focus Rubric (p.170)
Student Self Evaluation: Story In Art 3-5 (p.118)

(from painting The Persistence of Memory by Salvador Dali)

STORY PLANNING – ART CONNECTION

Group Members' Names:

TITLE:

SETTING: (Where does the story take place?)

CHARACTERS: (Who is in the story?)

WHAT, IN OUR ART WORK, INSPIRES OUR STORY?
1. Images:

2. Mood:

3. Colors and shapes:

PLOT: (What happens in the story?)
1. BEGINNING (Who and where are the characters and what are their relationships?):

2. MIDDLE (What problem develops for the main character to solve?):

3. END (How does the character solve the problem?):

WORK PLAN: (List of who will construct each puppet and prop. Use back if needed.)
NAME: JOB:

Name _____ Date _____

How Did I Do?
STORY IN ART (GRADES K - 2)

AS A THINKER
1. I looked carefully at the painting for story ideas.

       *   ***   *****

2. I kept my story idea connected to the images in the painting.

       *   ***   *****

AS AN ART MAKER
3. I did my best to complete a puppet that looked like it belonged in the painting.

       *   ***   *****

AS A PERFORMER
4. I cooperated with my class members to present our story idea.

       *   ***   *****

5. I took the performance seriously and did my best to bring my character to life.

       *   ***   *****

AS AN AUDIENCE MEMBER
6. I watched the shows quietly.

       *   ***   *****

7. I gave polite and thoughtful comments about other stories.

       *   ***   *****

_____

8. My thoughts on the experience (use back of paper if needed):

Name _____ Date _____

How Did I Do?
STORY IN ART (GRADES 3 - 5)

AS A THINKER
1. I looked for imagery in the painting for story ideas.

       *   ***   *****

2. I worked with my partners to complete the Story Planning Page.

       *   ***   *****

3. I worked with my partners to plan our presentation.

       *   ***   *****

AS AN ART MAKER
4. I helped complete the scenery and puppets for our presentation.

       *   ***   *****

AS A PERFORMER
5. I cooperated with my partners to present the work we had created.

       *   ***   *****

6. I did not take any script on stage, but improvised the script based on our plan.

       *   ***   *****

7. I took the performance seriously and did my best to bring my character to life.

       *   ***   *****

8. I listened to the critique.

       *   ***   *****

AS AN AUDIENCE MEMBER
9. I watched the shows quietly.

       *   ***   *****

10. I gave polite and thoughtful comments in critique.

       *   ***   *****

_____

11. My thoughts on the experience (use back of paper if needed):

Name _____ Date _____

How Did I Do?
CONFLICT RESOLUTION

AS A THINKER
1. I worked with my group to create three different conflict resolutions.

       *   ***   *****

2. I worked with my group to complete the Story Planning Sheet.

       *   ***   *****

3. I worked with my group to plan our presentation.

       *   ***   *****

AS AN ART MAKER
4. I completed the puppets required for our presentation.

       *   ***   *****

AS A PERFORMER
5. I cooperated with my group to present the work we had created.

       *   ***   *****

6. I did not take any script on stage, but improvised the script based on our plan.

       *   ***   *****

7. I took the performance seriously and did my best to bring my character to life.

       *   ***   *****

8. I listened to the critique.

       *   ***   *****

AS AN AUDIENCE MEMBER
9. I watched the shows quietly.

       *   ***   *****

10. I gave polite and thoughtful comments in critique.

       *   ***   *****

_____

11. My thoughts on the experience (use back of paper if needed):

LESSON FIFTEEN: THE CHOICE IS YOURS
Driving Question: What are our choices in the way we resolve a conflict?

Grades: 3 - 5

Overview
Students collaborate in creating solutions to realistic stories involving conflict choosing one of three endings: win/lose, lose/lose/, or win/win, then build puppets to perform their stories.

Time: Three – four 45 minute class sessions

ORGANIZE AND PREPARE

1. **SELECT** a puppet technique and gather materials.
QUICKEST: Shadow Puppets (p.155)
LONGER: Hand Puppets: Recycled Bottle Head, Rod Puppet: any two rod style
I have used shadow puppets by far the most for this project, as they are relatively quick to make and the simple black and white images lend themselves to realistic, serious stories in which unintended humor is not an asset. However, if the students are focused and mature enough to not be distracted by possibly funny-looking puppets, and still appreciate the intent of the story, any technique is fine.
Another option would be to use any classroom collection of puppets - either from previous projects, or purchased - as the performers of the stories.

2. **PRINT**:
• EITHER the eight Story Problem Planning Pages (p.124-131), OR copies of the blank Story Planning Page (p.123) (one/group)
The Story Problem Planning Pages contain a story seed: a problem for which the group must invent three endings to allow the students to immediately tackle the focus issue. Other options allow the teacher to assign specific seeds, or allow students to create their own problems around which to build the three different endings.

CORE STANDARDS:
Social Studies:
Civics: Government and Citizenship
Language Arts:
Reading for Informational Text: Key Ideas and Details; Integration of Knowledge and Ideas
Speaking and Listening: Comprehension and Collaboration; Presentation of Knowledge and Ideas

EXPECTED LEARNING OUTCOMES:
Students will be able to differentiate among three approaches to the resolution of a conflict.
Students will be able to dramatize scenarios applying conscious choices in conflict resolution.
Students will be able to evaluate options in conflict resolution as applied to real life.

VOCABULARY:

compromise: a way of settling a conflict in which everyone agrees to be flexible on what they want

conflict: a disagreement

Win/lose: a conflict resolution in which one person gets what they want and the other does not

Lose/lose: a conflict resolution in which neither person gets what they want

Win/win: a conflict resolution in which both people get what they want

resolution: an answer or solution to a problem

- Check List for selected puppet technique (one/group) (Section IV)
- Project Self Evaluation – one/student (p.119)
- Teamwork & Focus Rubric - one/student (p.170)

INTRODUCE

People, even countries, have disagreements every day that require solutions. In many stories we see, whoever is stronger gets what they want, and the weaker one loses. This is called a win/lose resolution.

Can you think of a story like this? Have you had a disagreement in real life end this way?

But this is not the only way conflicts are resolved. Sometimes something may happen in which neither party gets what they want. This is called a lose/lose resolution.
Can you think of a real life example of this?

And sometimes, with real thought and effort, both parties can get what they want, to have a win/win resolution. This should be the goal of any conflict resolution. This solution may require compromise, or both parties agreeing on something slightly different from their original goal.

You are going to work with partners to create a story with three possible endings: win/lose, lose/lose, and win/win. Once your three endings are written, you will make puppets to perform these stories.

Each group will need one writer, who listens to everyone's ideas and writes them down on the Story Development Page. Notice that there is very little space for writing. You are to write down ONLY the main ideas of your story, NOT a script, or every word that is spoken. The purpose of this page is to agree on the story, so that in performance, you can improvise the dialogue to tell this story.

Every group will also receive a Project Check List. We will read it together now. So, you see that this list includes all the steps needed to complete the project as well as tips to effectively use your puppets.
Each group will choose a Check List Manager. This person's job is to check off each step as it is finished. When it is time to rehearse your story, you may ask a member of

RATIONALE FOR SHORT WRITING FORMAT

In performance, the story dialogue is improvised because:

- The Planning Page is not allowed backstage, to allow total focus on puppet manipulation – impossible if reading at the same time.
- Improvisation during performance requires immediate response to character emotions and motivations and fosters acute listening, thinking, and response skills.
- Many classes include students with a spectrum of reading abilities so no script reading is required. Reading ability has no connection to creative thinking or performance skills.
- Script memorization takes time better spent on performance skills. If you prefer complete scripts written and memorized, the Story Planning Page is still an effective place to begin.

The **Story Planning Page** facilitates:
- Construction of a cohesive story
- Agreement among group members on story events
- A written record of the group's plan, to be referred to and adhered to
- A simple framework on which improvised dialogue is based in performance

About 30 minutes is recommended for story writing to encourage students to quickly focus and work together, and to prevent writing a word for word script.

121

another group to be your director. The Director will look at the Performance Elements on this list and watch your show to help and advise you on clear story telling and effective puppet use.

FOCUS

1. Student groups of 3 - 5 students are assigned, or select, a real life, familiar problem around which to build a story, using EITHER one of the eight Story Problem Planning Pages, OR a blank Story Planning Page
2. Groups complete their story with three different endings.

CREATE

Make puppets as needed to tell story.

REHEARSE

1. Students organize puppets and props and practice with their group.
2. Students perform work for the class, with class Constructive Critique (p.171).

SHARE

Schedule a performance:
- for younger classes
- for classes doing the same project, to compare and contrast results
- for parents at an open house or other event
- as a designated teaching opportunity for other classes, open to post performance discussion

TIP: Small audiences are best so that puppeteers' voices may be heard, unless amplification is available that does not necessitate leaning in to a microphone.

REFLECT

How can individuals control their response to conflict? Did you have any conflicts within your group during this project? How did you resolve them? Can you think of any family, school, community, national, or international conflicts that would benefit from thoughtful conflict resolution?

ASSESS

Teacher: Performance based as well as Teamwork & Focus Rubric (p.170)
Student: Self Evaluation: Conflict Resolution (p.119)

STORY PLANNING PAGE

PLOT: The events that happen in a story

The BEGINNING should answer the following questions:
Who is the ONE main character? Are there other characters they know? When and where does the story take place? What does the main character want?

The MIDDLE is the main conflict of the story.
What problem(s) keeps the main character from getting what they want?

The END resolves the conflict.
Does the main character succeed at getting what they want?
1. Win/Lose Ending:

2. Lose/Lose Ending:

3. Win/Win Ending:

SETTING: Where does the story take place?

WHO is the MAIN CHARACTER?
WHO are the other characters?

TITLE: Title of your group's story

CONSTRUCTION PLAN: Who will make each puppet or prop?

Group Members' Names	Group Members' Jobs
1.	1.
2.	2.
3.	3.
4.	4.
5.	5.

CONFLICT # 1

PLOT: The events that happen in a story
The BEGINNING should answer the following questions:
Who is the main character? Are there other characters they know? When and where does the story take place? What does the main character want?
Two siblings' aunt bought them a new toy.

The MIDDLE is the main conflict of the story.
What problem(s) keeps the main character from getting what they want?
They both want to be first to play with it.

The END resolves the conflict.
Does the main character succeed at getting what they want?
1. Win/Lose Ending:

2. Lose/Lose Ending:

3. Win/Win ending:

SETTING: Where does the story take place?

WHO is the MAIN CHARACTER? **a child**
WHO are the other characters? **child's sister or brother, their aunt**

TITLE: Title of your group's story: The New Toy
CONSTRUCTION PLAN: Who will make each puppet or prop?

Group Members' Names	Group Members' Jobs
1.	1.
2.	2.
3.	3.
4.	4.
5.	5.

CONFLICT # 2

PLOT: The events that happen in a story

The BEGINNING should answer the following questions:

Who is the main character? Are there other characters they know? When and where does the story take place? What does the main character want?

A student needs to use the kitchen table to work on a school project.

The MIDDLE is the main conflict of the story.

What problem(s) keeps the main character from getting what they want?

The student's little sister and her friend want to play a game there.

The END resolves the conflict.

Does the main character succeed at getting what they want?

1. Win/Lose Ending:

2. Lose/Lose Ending:

3. Win/Win ending:

SETTING: Where does the story take place?

WHO is the MAIN CHARACTER? **a student**
WHO are the other characters? **student's sister or brother, their friend, their mother**

TITLE: Title of your group's story: The Table
CONSTRUCTION PLAN: Who will make each puppet or prop?

Group Members' Names	Group Members' Jobs
1.	1.
2.	2.
3.	3.
4.	4.
5.	5.

CONFLICT # 3

PLOT: The events that happen in a story
The BEGINNING should answer the following questions:
Who is the main character? Are there other characters they know? When and where does the story take place? What does the main character want?
A child is shooting baskets on the playground.

The MIDDLE is the main conflict of the story.
What problem(s) keeps the main character from getting what they want?
Another child joins in but won't give the ball back.

The END resolves the conflict.
Does the main character succeed at getting what they want?
1. Win/Lose Ending:

2. Lose/Lose Ending:

3. Win/Win ending:

SETTING: Where does the story take place?

WHO is the MAIN CHARACTER? **Child # 1**
WHO are the other characters? **Child # 2, an adult**

TITLE: Title of your group's story: Basketball
CONSTRUCTION PLAN: Who will make each puppet or prop?

Group Members' Names	Group Members' Jobs
1.	1.
2.	2.
3.	3.
4.	4.
5.	5.

CONFLICT # 4

PLOT: The events that happen in a story
The BEGINNING should answer the following questions:
Who is the main character? Are there other characters they know? When and where does the story take place? What does the main character want?
Two friends have been playing outside and are thirsty.

The MIDDLE is the main conflict of the story.
What problem(s) keeps the main character from getting what they want?
They only have enough money for one cold drink.

The END resolves the conflict.
Does the main character succeed at getting what they want?
1. Win/Lose Ending:

2. Lose/Lose Ending:

3. Win/Win ending:

SETTING: Where does the story take place?

WHO is the MAIN CHARACTER? **Child # 1**
WHO are the other characters? **Child # 2, store owner**

TITLE: Title of your group's story: Thirsty Two
CONSTRUCTION PLAN: Who will make each puppet or prop?

Group Members' Names	Group Members' Jobs
1.	1.
2.	2.
3.	3.
4.	4.
5.	5.

CONFLICT # 5

PLOT: The events that happen in a story

The BEGINNING should answer the following questions:

Who is the main character? Are there other characters they know? When and where does the story take place? What does the main character want?

One student did their homework but their friend didn't.

The MIDDLE is the main conflict of the story.

What problem(s) keeps the main character from getting what they want?

The friend wants to copy the student's homework, which is against school rules.

The END resolves the conflict.

Does the main character succeed at getting what they want?

1. Win/Lose Ending:

2. Lose/Lose Ending:

3. Win/Win ending:

SETTING: Where does the story take place?

WHO is the MAIN CHARACTER? **Child # 1**
WHO are the other characters? **Child # 2, teacher**

TITLE: Title of your group's story: **Homework**
CONSTRUCTION PLAN: Who will make each puppet or prop?

Group Members' Names	Group Members' Jobs
1.	1.
2.	2.
3.	3.
4.	4.
5.	5.

CONFLICT # 6

PLOT: The events that happen in a story
The BEGINNING should answer the following questions:
Who is the main character? Are there other characters they know? When and where does the story take place? What does the main character want?
On child is playing at a friend's house.

The MIDDLE is the main conflict of the story.
What problem(s) keeps the main character from getting what they want?
The friend says the child has to come with them to a playground the child is not allowed to go to.

The END resolves the conflict.
Does the main character succeed at getting what they want?
1. Win/Lose Ending:

2. Lose/Lose Ending:

3. Win/Win ending:

SETTING: Where does the story take place?

WHO is the MAIN CHARACTER? **Child # 1**
WHO are the other characters? **Child # 2, parent**

TITLE: Title of your group's story: **The Playground**
CONSTRUCTION PLAN: Who will make each puppet or prop?

Group Members' Names	Group Members' Jobs
1.	1.
2.	2.
3.	3.
4.	4.
5.	5.

CONFLICT # 7

PLOT: The events that happen in a story

The BEGINNING should answer the following questions:

Who is the main character? Are there other characters they know? When and where does the story take place? What does the main character want?

The present a child's sister would like for her birthday costs $5.

The MIDDLE is the main conflict of the story.

What problem(s) keeps the main character from getting what they want?

The child has only five dollars and at the store, they see something that they really want that also costs $5.

The END resolves the conflict.

Does the main character succeed at getting what they want?

1. Win/Lose Ending:

2. Lose/Lose Ending:

3. Win/Win ending:

SETTING: Where does the story take place?

WHO is the MAIN CHARACTER? **Child # 1**
WHO are the other characters? **sister, store manager**

TITLE: Title of your group's story: **Shopping**
CONSTRUCTION PLAN: Who will make each puppet or prop?

Group Members' Names	Group Members' Jobs
1.	1.
2.	2.
3.	3.
4.	4.
5.	5.

CONFLICT # 8

PLOT: The events that happen in a story

The BEGINNING should answer the following questions:

Who is the main character? Are there other characters they know? When and where does the story take place? What does the main character want?

A child is playing with other children on a playground.

The MIDDLE is the main conflict of the story.

What problem(s) keeps the main character from getting what they want?

One child keeps teasing another because they cannot run fast.

The END resolves the conflict.

Does the main character succeed at getting what they want?

1. Win/Lose Ending:

2. Lose/Lose Ending:

3. Win/Win ending:

SETTING: Where does the story take place?

WHO is the MAIN CHARACTER? **Child # 1**
WHO are the other characters? **Child # 2, Child # 1**

TITLE: Title of your group's story: **Teasing**
CONSTRUCTION PLAN: Who will make each puppet or prop?

Group Members' Names	Group Members' Jobs
1.	1.
2.	2.
3.	3.
4.	4.

PUPPET MAKING TECHNIQUES

PERFORMANCE CONSIDERATIONS

It is crucial to know your end goal from the beginning: to select the puppet technique based on the number and age of students involved, along with resources, time, and space available and planned audience for finished work.

Following are a few ideas and suggestions:

For intimate classroom performances:
Staging:
May be from complex to no staging at all (tabletop, finger puppets), or a variety of individual stage options (toy theater, hand held finger puppet stage)

For performances in classroom, library, hallway, etc. for visiting class:
Staging: May be more complex, but NOT heavy. May be cardboard construction built just for this show from appliance boxes, etc.
Puppeteers: Ten – twenty, depending on back stage space. Students will have to understand that they must make space for others immediately when their scene is finished.
Puppets: A wide variety of possibilities and combinations, including shadow if the light accommodates. A variety of sizes of puppets are effective, as long as the audience is not large (one class at a time).
Sound: Small audiences are best so that puppeteers' voices may be heard, unless amplification is available that does not necessitate leaning in to a microphone. Of course, wireless headset microphones are ideal, but costly. Better to do multiple performances for small audiences than to push the limits of performers' voices.

For School Assembly
Staging: May be complex or simple as desired. Since it will not have to be portable, more complex designs are possible, but all must be a large enough scale to be seen. Or, use no staging at all for a Parade Puppet presentation. Complex or professional quality staging is beyond the scope of this book, but there are many online resources.
Puppeteers: Entire class or more, as space allows and program necessitates.
Puppets: All must be medium to large scale, for visibility
Sound: Back stage microphones are necessary, UNLESS a downstage narrator (with a microphone) narrates as the puppets' movement illustrates the story.

Evening Family event or Classroom tour
Staging: very simple, sturdy and portable. If it must be disassembled to be moved, very quick and simple.
Puppeteers: five – ten in each cast
Puppets: light weight, plan how they will be transported. Rolling suitcases work well. Or, if a small, simple production, each child may carry their own puppet.
Sound considerations as above, depending on expected audience size.

NO MARIONETTES?

You will note that there is no mention of marionettes, or string puppets in any lessons in this book. That is, for one reason, because I have used them very little in my own work as I have always preferred to have a more direct, physical connection with the puppet. Every puppeteer has their own personal preferences, just as most musicians devote themselves to certain instruments. Another reason I have rarely used marionettes in student workshops is because I seek simple and versatile techniques with maximum natural control and minimum distraction, which can quickly lead to dramatic expression to support the over arching goals of each project. Building and learning to operate a marionette is an excellent exercise in creative engineering, as a study in balance, materials, and patience and there are other books on this topic.

A NOTE ABOUT NOSES

An exaggerated nose is one of the most important features for any puppet. The nose gives focus to the puppet's gaze - so the audience can more easily tell where the puppet is looking. **DON'T FORGET THE NOSE!**

USE WHAT YOU HAVE

Puppets have always been constructed of whatever material is available, so look around and see what you can find for free. At a workshop I led in Chennai, India, for children, paper was not easily available, but we made puppets of gorgeous silk scraps from the tailors. At a workshop for puppeteers in Cordoba, Argentina, we scavenged plastic bottles and found sticks in the woods to construct highly articulated puppets using all free materials. At schools with no art budget at all, my students have brought in empty cereal boxes to make dynamic puppets they couldn't wait to take home.

From The Elephant's Child by Rudyard Kipling: puppets made by author from old sweaters

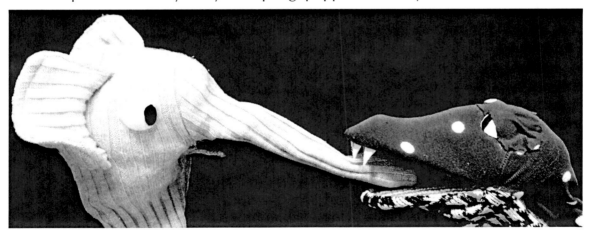

FINGER PUPPETS

Finger puppets are made in many parts of the world. One especially refined tradition comes from Guatemala, where colorful, detailed puppets are knit featuring people as well as animals of all kinds, particularly the indigenous animals of the country.

IN PERFORMANCE

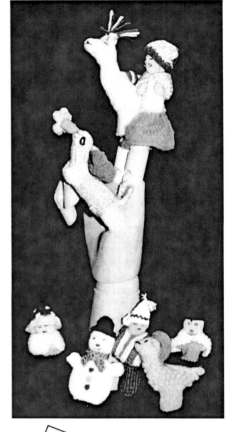

Finger puppets can appear from behind a book or out of a pocket. Or they can use no stage at all and come to life in the human scale world: the Paper Walkers can explore a map or act out a story on a tabletop. The Paper Tube finger puppets can line up behind each other and measure (as 1" inch worms) for a math project. Or a portable stage can go anywhere.

Finger puppets are best used for informal presentations or simple stories and songs for and by younger children, individually, or in small groups.

Advise younger children to hold down fingers without puppets with the thumb.

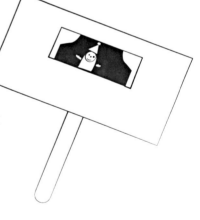

PORTABLE STAGE
- Cut stage opening in approx. 6"x10" (15-25cm) cardboard
- Glue or tape fabric scrap curtain across top of hole on back
- Glue and/or tape craft stick handle to back
* Hold handle with one hand, operate puppet with other.

PAPER TUBE
- poster board, cardstock, or recycled file folder cut appox. 3" x 3" (8x8cm)
- glue and/or tape
- construction paper scraps
- pointy markers
- scissors

Optional: very small wiggly eyes

TO MAKE:
1. Roll paper around finger, just tight enough so it does not slip off
2. Apply drop of glue and tape.
3. Decorate by adding a paper face, wings, tail, arms, etc.

STUFFED FABRIC

- Soft fabric circle cut about 8-10" (20-25cm) diameter
- Strong rubber band - about 4" (10cm) diameter
- small wad of polyfil stuffing (or waded plastic grocery bag, or paper)
- Strong paper or felt scraps (for youngest children, pre-cut in 1" (2.5cm) circles)
- Fabric scraps & yarn
* craft glue, or glue gun
- scissors

TO MAKE:

1. Place stuffing material in center of circle.
2. Wrap fabric around it and secure with rubber band, creating a ball shape in center of fabric. **Make sure rubber band is left loose enough that a finger can be inserted from below.**
3. Glue approx. 1" (2.5c m) circles of poster board to head as face.
4. Decorate with pointed markers OR use felt circle, small wiggly eyes, and small felt scraps to create a face.
5. Add yarn or fabric scraps for hair.

GLOVE FINGER

- Mate-less or thrift store gloves
- Craft glue thinned with water
- Decorating materials as in Sewn Felt Form Puppet.

TO MAKE:

1. Cut fingers off gloves.
2. Dip cut end in glue to prevent unraveling.
3. Allow to dry.
4. Decorate.

SEWN FELT FORM

- Two of pattern cut from felt, fleece, or other sturdy material
- sewing tools OR hot glue gun
- felt scraps for faces (for youngest children, pre-cut in 1" (2.5cm) circles)
- felt scraps, wiggly eyes, yarn, etc., for decoration
- craft glue
- scissors

TO MAKE:

1. With right sides in, sew or hot glue close to edge.
2. **Turn right side out.**
3. OR with right sides out, sew with decorative or matching color close to edge and leave as is.
4. Decorate with felt scraps, etc.

1.

2.

3 & 4.

Sewn or Glued
Finger
Puppet
Pattern

CUT 2

DO NOT SEW HERE

PAPER WALKERS

- 3" x 5" (7.5x12.5cm) file card, or file folder pieces
- thin rubber band approx. 3" (7.5cm) diameter
- masking tape
- markers, crayons, or colored pencils

TO MAKE:

1. Decorate paper with a whole body, head and arms drawn on, the bottom of the rectangle being the lower edge of the hips. NO LEGS!

2. Tape a rubber band crosswise on back near bottom end of rectangle. OPTIONAL: Add paper arms that stick out. Cut out around head shape. Staple or glue on yarn hair.

TO OPERATE:

3. With palm facing down and puppet's head pointing AWAY FROM fingertips, put all four fingers through rubber band.

4. Form hand position as for a "peace" sign, with thumb holding two folded fingers down.

5. Keeping hand in this position, raise hand angle to vertical, resting on the two extended fingertips.

The particularly dextrous may use their thumb and little finger sticking out as arms.

These are extremely simple and quick to make, and amazingly engaging for all ages! They can dance, explore maps, live in shoebox houses...

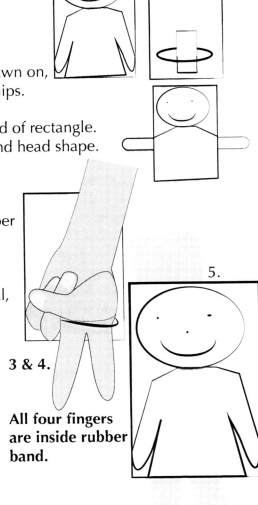

1.

2.

3 & 4.

All four fingers are inside rubber band.

5.

GLOVE STORY PUPPET

(usually for adult storytelling use)

- one glove
- decorating materials as in Sewn Felt Form Puppet.

A knit glove can be used by an adult to present a whole story cast, with each finger decorated as a character from the same story.

Bend fingers up and down for characters' entrances and exits and wiggle to indicate speech.

HAND PUPPETS

Hand puppets have traditions all over the world. Punch and Judy are hand puppet characters from Great Britain famous for mocking the powerful, with puppet relatives in Italy, Germany, Poland, and more. Chinese hand puppets are manipulated in a highly refined acrobatic technique. Argentina's beloved poet and playwrite Javier Villafañe began as a puppeteer. Puppets shown are Pulchinella (Italy) by Brina Babini and contemporary character from China, and from Costa Rica (right) by Hilda D. Gonzáles Barrantes.

IN PERFORMANCE

Hand puppets communicate through movement, as human actions and emotions are expressed through movements of the fingers, wrist, and arm. See Hand and Rod Puppet Stages and Hand Puppet Movement pages for specific tips and exercises.

HAND EYES

1. Bend 12" (30cm) pipe cleaner in half. Now twist each end into a flat, tight spiral.
2. Hot glue 1/2" (1. 2cm) wiggly eye on each spiral.
3. Palm down, place middle finger at center bend, with eyes coming up between adjacent fingers, eyes facing tips of fingers.
4. Bend wrist with thumb below as the lower jaw, and start talking!

HEAD CONSTRUCTION OPTIONS

RECYCLED BOTTLE

- small, clean, plastic bottle, upside down, size so first or first and second fingers fit in bottle mouth. The smaller the hand, the smaller the bottle so it is not top heavy.
- misc. recycled or other decoration materials
- hot glue gun or craft glue

OPTIONAL: masking tape and paint, OR small sock OR T-shirt fabric

TO MAKE:

Decorate as is OR wrap first in masking tape and paint, OR cover first with small sock or T-shirt fabric, rubber-banded around bottle neck.

STUFFED SOCK OR FABRIC

- short, medium sized child sock OR soft fabric
- plastic shopping bag, or fabric scraps, or polyfill stuffing
- misc. recycled or other decoration materials: fabric, felt, pom-poms, eyes, yarn, etc.
- rubber band
- hot glue gun or craft glue

TO MAKE:

1. Stuff sock with wadded bag, scraps, or stuffing until it forms a nice oval – not too tightly stuffed.
2. Place a sturdy rubber band at the base of the shape and double, leaving it loose enough to put one or two fingers through.
3. Decorate the face, adding features and hair. Yarn wigs best attached with hot glue, or sewn.

NEWSPAPER AND MASKING TAPE

• newspaper
OPTIONAL: cardboard tube
• masking tape
* markers, paint, yarn, etc.

TO MAKE:

1. Ball newspaper sheet around one finger and have a partner wrap masking tape around the paper to hold the shape. OR start with a cardboard tube over finger and attach newspaper VERY securely to tube. Facial features can be pinched out of the newspaper, and extra elements can be added on – especially a prominent nose - using more tape.
2. Wrap completely with a final layer of tape.
3. Add details with paint, permanent markers, or glue.

BODY CONSTRUCTION OPTIONS

These puppet body designs may be used with any of the head construction options.

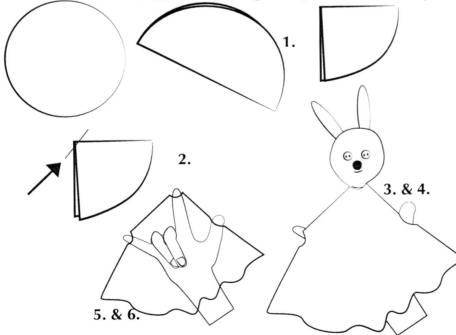

1.

2.

3. & 4.

5. & 6.

This is a very quick and simple design

FABRIC CIRCLE

• circle of soft fabric about 18″ (45cm) in diameter.

TO MAKE:

1. Fold circle in quarters to find center point.
2. Cut tiny hole at center. A finger should just fit through hole.
3. Insert puppet neck through hole and attach securely to fabric circle with craft or hot glue.
4. Place first finger through hole.
5. As pictured, stretch out thumb and little finger.
6. Cut VERY small hole where thumb and little finger touch fabric.
7. Insert finger and thumb tips through holes to be puppet hands.

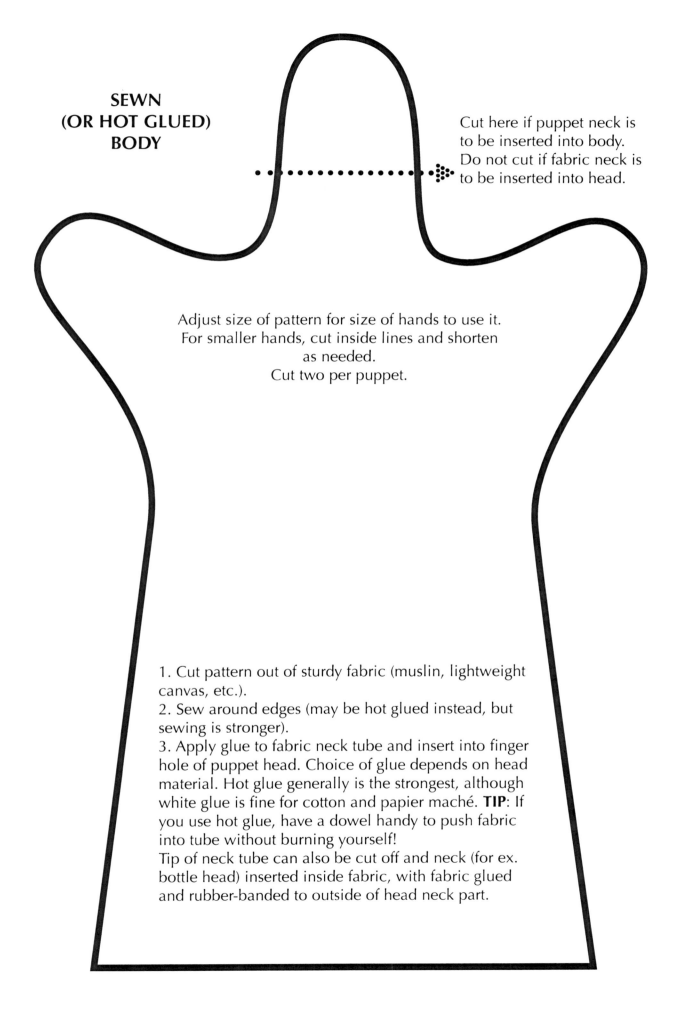

SEWN (OR HOT GLUED) BODY

Cut here if puppet neck is to be inserted into body. Do not cut if fabric neck is to be inserted into head.

Adjust size of pattern for size of hands to use it. For smaller hands, cut inside lines and shorten as needed.
Cut two per puppet.

1. Cut pattern out of sturdy fabric (muslin, lightweight canvas, etc.).
2. Sew around edges (may be hot glued instead, but sewing is stronger).
3. Apply glue to fabric neck tube and insert into finger hole of puppet head. Choice of glue depends on head material. Hot glue generally is the strongest, although white glue is fine for cotton and papier maché. **TIP**: If you use hot glue, have a dowel handy to push fabric into tube without burning yourself!
Tip of neck tube can also be cut off and neck (for ex. bottle head) inserted inside fabric, with fabric glued and rubber-banded to outside of head neck part.

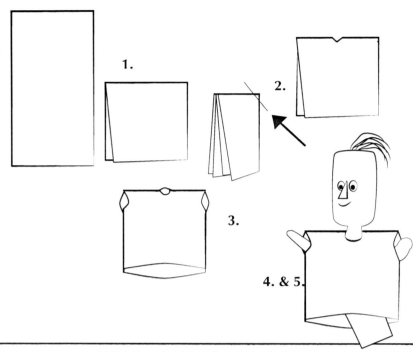

KAFTAN STYLE
- fabric rectangle approx. 6" x 18" (15x45cm)
- hot glue or sewing tools

TO MAKE:
1. Fold fabric in quarters.
2. Cut very small hole at fold point.
3. Folded in half, sew or glue sides together, leaving about 1" (2.5cm) open at fold end of seam for finger holes.
4. Attach puppet head at center fold hole with hot glue so that finger(s) can go through hole in fabric and into puppet head/neck.
5. Extend thumb and little finger through holes at top of seam as hands.

HEAD AND BODY TOGETHER CONSTRUCTION OPTIONS

PAPER PLATE PUPPET
- 1 and 1/2 paper plates
- stapler
- markers, crayons, craft glue, decoration materials

TO MAKE:
1. With bottom of plate up, decorate entire plate as a face.
2. Cut another plate in half.
3. With concave sides together, staple the ½ plate to back of the top half of the face, forming a pocket that a hand can be slipped into. **TIP:** Best to attach 1/2 plate AFTER decoration to assure face will be right side up!
4. Attach a piece of construction paper or fabric at the bottom, to serve as simple body, as well as to hide arm.

STUFFED ANIMAL TRANSFORMATION
With minimal to no sewing, a thrift store stuffed animal can become an effective hand puppet. Choose one not too small, or large, for your hand. Look for one with the ends of the arms NOT sewn flat into the side seam, as you will not be able to put your fingers into the arms. Open the seam near the tail end of the animal and remove enough stuffing to allow space for your hand. If the puppet is to be used for a small audience, the face may be fine as is. For a large audience, you may need to add larger eyes. Pictured puppets made from author's grandmother's bear collection.

SOCK MOUTH PUPPET
- ankle sock that fits comfortably over hand
- craft glue or glue gun
- pom-poms, wiggly eyes, misc. decoration materials
- scissors

TO MAKE:

1. Place hand in sock, with fingertips where toes would go and thumb at knitted corner where heel would go (tube socks are NOT recommended).

2. Glue two pompoms just in front of knuckles (towards finger tips).

3. Glue two ½ - ¾ " (1.2-1.9cm) wiggly eyes to pompoms so that they face FORWARD toward the finger tips, NOT on top looking up. This allows the puppet to naturally look at the audience.

4. Glue details with felt scraps: white glue if puppet will have time to dry before using - otherwise, hot glue.

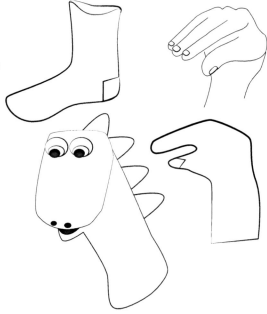

SOCK FULL BODY PUPPET
- short "no show" or tube sock
- felt circle about 3" (7.6cm) in diameter
- yarn
- wiggly eyes, misc. fabric scraps, ribbon, etc.
- scissors
- craft glue or glue gun

1. Place sock on the table, flattening it to make a symmetrical shape (without the heel sticking out to one side). Turn sock over so heel is hidden.

2. Cut a felt circle about 3" (7.6cm) in diameter and glue to sock very close to the toe end. That will be the face. Decorate with features cut from felt, wiggly eyes, etc.

3. Add **YARN WIG** - MUCH easier to make wig than glue separate strands of yarn hair: Wind yarn about 10 times around a small book or other form. Cut extra yarn length and tie tightly around wound yarn. Remove from form and hold up by knot. Cut at opposite side of yarn circle. Hot glue knotted part to puppet's head. Braid or style as desired.

4. With small fabric scraps, add clothes. DO NOT wrap cloth all the way around sock, as the fabric will not allow the sock to stretch to insert hand.

5. Finally, put sock on hand and mark where thumb and little finger are. Remove sock and make TINY snip with scissors (tiny because knit sock stretches) at thumb and little finger joint.

6. Put sock back on hand and extend thumb and little finger through holes in sock as hands/arms.

HAND PUPPET MOVEMENT

Hand puppets are generally worn with the palm of the hand facing to the front, to allow the fingers to bend forward as the puppet's arms and hands.

Movements of a puppet do not need to totally parallel human movement as they strive to express human action and emotion. Certain movements are very "puppety", in other words, movements only a puppet would, or could, do, but we interpret them in human terms anyway.

CROSSING THE STAGE

Hold the arm so that it is vertical from the elbow up. When the puppet moves horizontally to walk, the arm should remain vertical and not slant over. Move from the shoulder!

For most professional looking movement: Rather than lifting the fingers, keep the fingers rigid and drop the thumb. This takes practice!

The puppeteer's wrist moves as the puppet's hips.

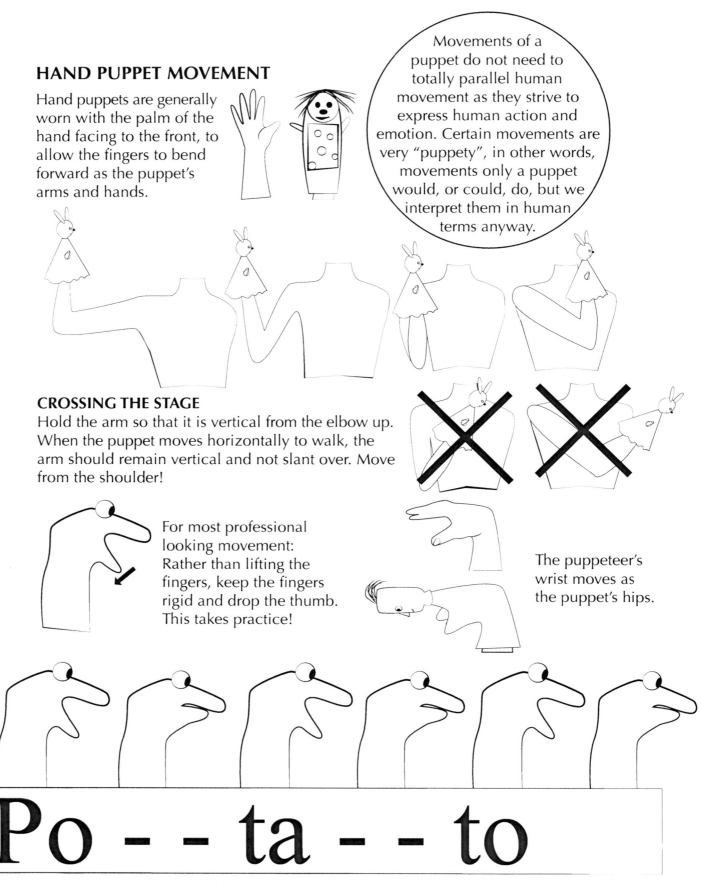

Po - - ta - - to

Mouth puppets should match the movement of the mouth to the words – with the mouth opening for each syllable.

Specific expressive movements can be performed using fingers alone, wrist alone, or arm alone. Take a few minutes to practice these movements together when puppets are completed!

FINGER MOVEMENTS:
- nodding head
- pointing at self
- motioning "come here"
- pointing
- waving
- rubbing hands
- washing face
- thinking (as resting chin on hand)
- creeping (since a hand puppet has no feet, it may use its hands to slowly creep across the playboard to sneak up on something)
- crying
- sneezing
- snoring - human heads do not move while sleeping, but for effect, a puppet's may.

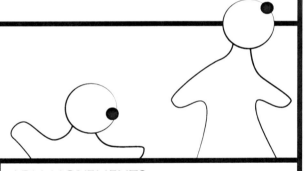

WRIST MOVEMENTS:
- shaking head no (because the finger cannot twist like the neck, a puppet must shake their whole body from the wrist)
- bowing
- looking side to side, up and down
- reading (for effect, the puppet moves its whole body side to side when reading),
- shy (twisting away from audience)
- sorrow (bending down)
- picking things up (bending from "waist")
- more exaggerated crying, sneezing (Cover your mouths, Puppets!), snoring

ARM MOVEMENTS:
- walking (We shift our weight from one foot to the other to walk, so the puppet moves slightly back and forth as it moves forward.)
- running
- hopping
- skipping
- fainting (silly movement as puppet may pivot in a circle from elbow until whole puppet falls over)
- falling
- flying
- REALLY exaggerated crying, sneezing, snoring

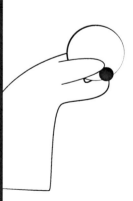

QUICK HAND OR ROD PUPPET STAGE IDEAS

Sturdy, collapsible stage frames can be constructed with PVC plumbing tubing and fittings, then covered with fabric attached with Velcro. Foldable wood puppet theaters are also an option. Included here are some instant and inexpensive options to use right away.
You may find other options: a free standing bookshelf? a row of chairs covered with fabric?

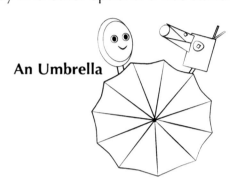

An Umbrella

NOTE:
The space on the audience side of the curtain is for **PUPPETS ONLY!**
It is important to keep that space for the magical world of the puppets, and NOT for human faces.

A Table on its Side
NOTE: It may be most stable to point table legs towards audience because puppeteers are likely to lean on table. Check design of your table to see which way is safest.
A narrow board may be secured across table legs as a prop shelf.

A Spring Curtain Rod
across a doorway with a curtain

OR, better yet, two spring curtain rods with a sheer scrim curtain on top to conceal the faces of standing puppeteers

A Rolling Clothes Rack, available at housewares stores, can support a curtain for taller students, or can support a scrim and lower curtain for smaller students.

Scrim:
A sheer dark color or black curtain allows some concealment of puppeteers' faces but allows puppeteers to see movement of their puppets. Most effective without strong light behind the puppeteers.

Folded cardboard stores easily and can be decorated as a stage. Available at fabric stores as temporary cutting surface, OR use packing tape and double ply cardboard sheets to construct this.

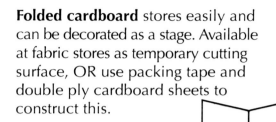

Cardboard Box Stages
Medium size box placed on table: Cut performance space (proscenium) hole on one side of box and cut out opposite side. Cut away half of bottom to allow space for puppeteers' arms. Tape box at edge of table to keep from moving.

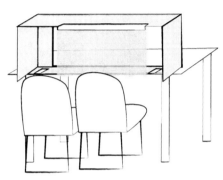

Back stage view:
Children may sit in chairs or stand to operate puppets.

MASKS

Masks have been used world-wide for thousands of years and are related to puppets through the "willing suspension of disbelief" basic to the use of both, as well as to spiritual and ritual connections.

A mask may simply neutralize the wearer's face, as this mask from the current New York Sleep No More participatory theater production, or change the wearer into something else, as this traditional Mexican diablo mask, or the contemporary star mask by Gabrare Q.

Versatile Paper Plate Mask

- budget quality paper plates (1 per student)
- hole punch
- scissors
- masking tape
- stapler
- rubber bands 3" (7.6cm) diameter (2 per student)

OPTIONAL: Decorate mask with markers, feathers, fabric. etc.

Bear mask made by author from milk jug

1. Fold paper plate in half, concave side in.

2. About 1/3 distance from either end of fold, push fold as far as possible into hole punch and punch through both layers.

3. On desk, NOT LAP, insert point of scissors into holes to cut larger - just big enough to see through.

4. At about 1/3 distance from other end of fold, make about 1 inch (2.5cm) cut perpendicular to fold.

5. Cut along fold from this end up to perpendicular cut. Unfold and you have a cut shaped like the letter "T".

6. Open plate and slide one flap over other, causing fold to come forward to form a nose. Staple overlapping flaps.

7. With masking tape, attach rubber bands to edge of plate, sticking out next to each eye hole. These will be placed over ears to wear mask. OR, use strip of strong paper or fabric scrap to make headband attached to rubber bands.

IN PERFORMANCE: Remember when wearing a mask that the whole body should express this character.

The Sorcerer's Apprentice miming puppet constructed by author

MIMING PUPPETS

Miming puppets is a name for the style that involves a fairly close to life-size puppet, with the puppeteer's hand serving as the actual hand of the puppet, either bare or gloved. This allows manipulation of life size props, as well as life like hand gesture with one hand only as the puppeteer's other hand animates the head.

IN PERFORMANCE

The staging may be very minimal, as the puppeteer is immediately behind the puppet. A proscenium stage may be used with a scrim curtain between the puppeteer and the puppet, hiding the puppeteer's face.

If the puppeteer's face is visible, it is crucial that the puppeteer focus at all times on the puppet and avoid eye contact with the audience.

The puppeteer holds the head with their non-dominant hand, and puts other arm in the sleeve to allow the dominant hand to be the hand of the puppet. The puppeteer's arm extends forward, with elbows held close together, to maintain the illusion of the puppet's body. These puppets are effective as historical figures introducing themselves, or in stories with few characters and in which scenery is not essential.

Bottle Head Puppet

- approx. gallon (3-4 liter) clean bottle (upside down to form head)
- paint stir stick
- cardboard
- lightweight, long sleeved, high collared (recycled) shirt
- glue gun, packing tape

1. Securely tape stick into bottle neck, forming control rod.
2. Cut cardboard approx. 8"x12" (20x30cm), grain parallel to longer side.
3. Cut hole in center and insert bottle neck and stick.
4. Curve cardboard to form shoulders, puppet nose facing forward.
5. Attach securely with tape and/or glue.
6. Glue facial features with cardboard, bottle caps, shredded plastic bag hair, etc.
7. Put shirt on shoulders and attach, hiding rod. Shirt neck may have to be gathered in by winding string around and gluing.
8. Cut hole in center of back of shirt, to insert one hand to hold control rod.
9. Cut arm slot in one sleeve (right, if puppeteer is right handed)

OPTIONAL: Mask Face/Fabric Circle Body

1. Make paper plate mask using sturdy plate OR cardboard circle.
2. Tape to paint stir.
3. Insert rod through hole in center of lightweight fabric about 24" (61cm) square.
4. Secure just beneath plate face.
5. Staple sides together on one side, forming sleeve hole.
6. Cut hole in center back of fabric to hold control rod.

PAGEANT AND PARADE PUPPETS

These large-scale puppets have been used for centuries all over the world for outdoor events of spiritual, political, or celebratory nature. Themed characters can simply be carried in a parade, or can be used to tell a simple story for a large-scale event, with puppeteers in full view, carrying the puppets. Bread and Puppet Theater and In the Heart of the Beast Puppet and Mask Theater are well known American companies using this technique. Parade King made by author.

IN PERFORMANCE:

No staging is needed – simply an open space, outdoors, or indoors with a high ceiling.

Three puppeteers are required for each puppet. It is more effective if the body pole is held a bit behind the hand poles. These puppets move in a slow and majestic manner, and teamwork is required to move them well. In construction, it is crucial that all materials are as lightweight as possible. This project works well for smaller children if constructing a smaller puppet for a short parade route, such a school hallway. Wind is a factor to be considered outdoors!

CARDBOARD FACE PARADE PUPPET

- corrugated cardboard, or poster board
- packing tape, hot glue, large stapler
- paint or collage materials
- 3 lightweight poles: bamboo or PVC pipe about 6" (1.8M) long
- VERY LIGHTWEIGHT fabric about 48" (1.2M) wide by a bit less than double the height of the puppet.

1. Cut cardboard in 2-3' (60-90cm) head shape AND two hands of similar size. The hands do not have to have 5 fingers – mitten hands, or 3-4 fingers are fine.
2. Cut large, protruding nose.
3. Attach nose in center of face with tape or hot glue.
4. Add LARGE facial features using paint or collage as follows: Paint cardboard with white glue thinned with water. Place paper shapes and paint over with glue. Experiment mixing colors by layering tissue paper. Make sure all edges are glued securely. Allow to dry thoroughly. *Collage decoration may be done as teams working together on the head and each hand.*
4. Securely attach poles to head and each hand using any combination of hot glue and strong tape.
5. Fold fabric in quarters and snip the fold point.
6. Insert head pole through hole and glue or wrap with string to firmly attach to rod.
7. Hot glue fabric to head, concealing pole.
OPTIONAL: add rectangular shoulder with center hole to attach to pole just below head.
8. Lay puppet head and cloth body flat and hot glue fabric to hand at each fold so that stick is hidden inside fabric and hand shows as puppet hand. **The hands should be attached with thumbs pointing UP!**

Nose: Cut then fold on lines and glue edge flaps to face. Make sure to leave a forehead!

Make sure hands are attached to poles so that thumbs point UP, or towards head, for natural appearance!

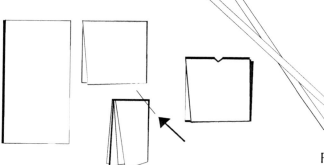

Fold and cut fabric center hole for pole

Fabric may be longer than pictured if sheer, or if cut in wide fringe so that puppeteers can see where they are going.

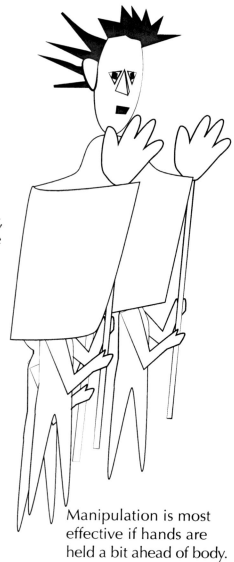

Manipulation is most effective if hands are held a bit ahead of body.

ROD PUPPETS

Supported and controlled by rods held by the puppeteer, diverse rod puppet traditions are world wide. Pictured, on right from the Bambara tradition of Mali is a folk character by Yaya Coulibaly. On left, from the ancient Wayang Golek tradition of Indonesia, a character rooted in ancient stories and spiritual beliefs. The horse is a contemporary puppet made in Costa Rica.

IN PERFORMANCE:

Rod puppet staging is similar to hand puppet staging, as the puppets are operated from below. A simple screen of any material is effective. With older puppeteers, and larger scale puppets, it can also be very effective to use no staging at all, so the audience sees the facial expressions of the puppeteers below the puppets held overhead. The simpler designs, for younger puppeteers, can also be without staging, as the puppet is used to very simply bring a character to life in the classroom. When featuring multiple puppets, clarify speaking puppet by giving it movement, with non-speaking puppet still.

Rod puppets can be very expressive in showing action and emotion through gesture. They cannot, however, pick up props, so the needs of the story should be considered when choosing this technique. Performance tips are similar to those of hand puppets.

DISPLAY:

If puppets are not going home immediately with students (ALWAYS the students preference), display by inserting rods into recycled Styrofoam, or hanging with clothespins to string. Please do not staple them to a bulletin board – this makes puppets very sad.

SINGLE ROD PUPPETS

BUTTERFLY
- 1 sheet colored paper
- craft stick
- markers, crayons
- craft glue

OPTIONAL: pipe cleaners for added legs and antennae, wiggly eyes

1. Cut butterfly wings as single shape by folding paper in half and cutting with body along fold.
2. Open and decorate with markers or crayons.
3. Glue near one end of craft stick, using protruding end of stick as control rod.
4. Add small wiggly eyes and pipe cleaner antennae if desired.

PAPER PLATE

- sturdy paper plate
- craft stick
- decoration materials
- fabric scrap

1. Decorate BOTTOM of plate as a face with markers, or glued paper
2. Tape craft stick as control rod.
3. Attach fabric scrap or paper at the bottom, as simple body, and to hide hand holding rod.

PAPER ASSEMBLED SHAPE

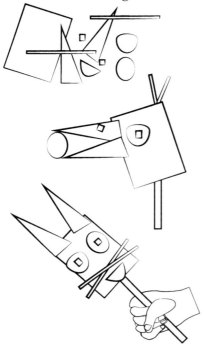

- cut or collected sturdy, varicolored paper shapes (5 – 10/ child)
- craft glue, staplers

1. Allow children to explore paper shapes and experiment on a flat surface, selecting a base shape for their character, and several small shapes for ears, horns, noses, hair, etc. Allow 5 – 10 minutes to experiment with shapes before offering glue.
2. Glue shapes together.

Glue sticks work, but create copious plastic waste. Better to buy gallon of glue and keep in tight lidded containers, for students to apply with cheapest, small paint brushes. Brushes easily washed.

Glue should dry quickly for immediate use if not applied excessively, otherwise, use stapler as needed.
3. Attach craft or popsicle stick as control rod with tape.
OPTIONAL: Attach a piece of construction paper or fabric at the bottom, to hide hand holding rod.

DOUBLE ROD PUPPETS

CATERPILLAR

- flexible foam packing material OR polyfoam cushion scrap approx. 1" x 1" x 8" (2.5x2.5x20cm)
- 2 popsicle sticks
- small decorations: scraps, glitter, toothpicks, wiggly eyes
- craft glue, hot glue

1. Cut small slit near each end of foam.
2. Insert popsicle stick in each slit, gluing with hot glue.
3. Decorate.
4. Animate by bringing rods apart and together.

FLAT HEAD

- 1 approx. 4" (10cm) circle of light cardboard or cardstock
- 2 approx. 2" (5cm) circles of light cardboard or cardstock and 1 popsicle stick OR small, flat wooden spoon (for hand)
- 1 craft stick
- lightweight fabric approx. 10" x 20" (25x50cm)
- craft glue, tape

1. Glue or tape larger circle to one end of craft stick.
2. Fold fabric in quarters and snip very small hole at fold point.
3. Insert stick into hole, gluing to conceal stick.
4. Glue small circles to each side of end of popsicle stick.
5. Lay puppet head and cloth body flat and glue popsicle stick so that stick is hidden inside fabric and circle shows as puppet hand (puppet will have only one hand).
6. Decorate with markers, construction paper scraps, wiggly eyes, yarn hair, etc. using craft glue.

WOODEN SPOON HEAD

Construct as above, using convex side of wooden cooking spoon as face, with spoon handle as control rod. You may find wooden teaspoons for the hand (one per puppet).

RECYCLED BOTTLE HEAD

- clean, recycled plastic water or other bottle
- approx. 8" (20cm) dowel
- soft, drapey fabric: circle about 18"(45cm) in diameter, or rectangle approx. 12" x 24" (30x60cm)
- misc. decorations: hot glue plastic parts, use craft glue for other materials

1. Insert dowel into bottle mouth and tape securely.
2. Decorate bottle (rod down) as is with facial features hot glued on, OR wrap first in masking tape (so paint will stick) and paint, then decorate.
3. Fold fabric in quarters to find center point and cut tiny hole at center.
4. Insert rod through hole and attach fabric with glue, tape, rubber band, or hot glue to neck of bottle, hiding rod inside fabric.
5. Cut 2 approx. 3-4" (8cm) hand shapes of poster board and glue to each side of end of another dowel, or use small wood or recycled plastic spoon.
6. Lay puppet head and cloth body flat and glue hand control rod so that stick is hidden inside fabric and hand shows as puppet hand. You may make this design with two hands, understanding that only one hand can be moved at a time unless a second puppeteer assists. When attaching hands, remember that it looks more natural for the thumbs to be pointing up!
7. Animate puppet with both hands hidden under fabric while holding rods.

This design can also be used with any of the head construction techniques in the hand puppet section. Whatever technique, the head must be very securely fastened to the rod.

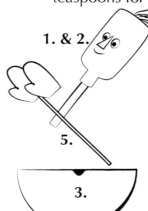

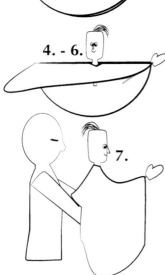

SHADOW PUPPETS

Indonesian wayang kulit:
Semar, a traditional wise
clown, on right.

Shadow puppetry originated in Asia about 2,000 years ago. Most often today, the puppeteer manipulates flat, opaque or translucent shapes against a translucent screen, generally lit from the side where the puppeteer works, with the audience watching the shadows on the other side. In Indonesia, however, the audience sits behind the puppeteer, watching his or (occasionally) her performance, which includes singing and deep knowledge of ancient stories, and features a gamelan orchestra of percussive instruments.

IN PERFORMANCE

Shadow puppets are an extremely versatile, simple, and magical technique for all ages. Puppets of simple or complex design come to life as excellent communicators. The puppet is held firmly against the screen from behind, grasping the rod as far from the puppet as possible to avoid causing a shadow of hand. Puppets enter and exit from one side of the screen rather than suddenly appearing in the center.

Puppet should move when speaking: when featuring multiple puppets, clarify speaking puppet by giving it movement, with non-speaking puppet still.

Puppet movement expresses story action. For an interesting presentation, the more focused action the better – **SHOW, DON'T TELL!**

NEEDED FOR ALL PROJECTS

LIGHT SOURCE

Lamp options:

• Single (two lamps may cause double shadow) clamp light clipped to top of screen frame, or to chair back or other support placed nearby

• Desk lamp with stand placed behind screen on table

LED and halogen lamps are preferable, but other bright lamps will work. For young children, place lamps with hot bulb high enough to avoid touching.

• Experiment with lamp placement to minimize shadows of rods.

SHADOW SCREEN

1. **SCREEN FRAME** options:

• Corrugated cardboard box or project board: stretch screen material over cut hole and attach with wide packing tape

• Canvas stretchers from art supply store: Attach foot on each end with "L" bracket and 1"x 2" (2.5x5cm) wood segment to stand frame on a table.

Attach screen to frame:
Stretch screen material gradually around frame, using staple gun.
OR, use sticky back Velcro.

2. **SHADOW SCREEN** material options:

• budget quality white plastic shower curtain *(author's favorite!)*

• white muslin

• medium weight paper (for small screens)

SHADOW PUPPET PLEDGE (courtesy of Hobey Ford, Goldenrod Puppets)
Highly recommended to avoid the construction of puppets too small
to attach rods to: *"Please raise your right hand and repeat after me:
I promise … I will not make … my puppet… smaller than my hand.
Now slap your hand down over your drawing.
If the drawing is hidden, it is too small."*

VOCABULARY
opaque - something light cannot pass through
perpendicular - at a 45 degree angle
profile - side view of a face
shadow screen - performance space for shadow puppets
translucent - something light passes through but cannot be seen through
transparent - something that can be seen through clearly (as glass)

SHADOW PUPPET MATERIALS
• BLACK construction paper (for non-jointed puppets),
poster board, or cardstock for jointed puppets cut in approx.
7" (17cm) squares
• Bendable straws for children under age 7, bamboo
skewers 7 and up
• Masking tape
• Brads (paper fasteners), OR string
• Glue (for Constructed Shape Puppets ONLY)
OPTIONAL:
• Colored clear plastic (clear colored report covers, cellophane wrapping paper, or theatrical
lighting gels (sometimes discarded by theaters)
* Paper doilies, netting, feathers

TOOLS:
* scissors
* Round hole punches
* Pencils (erasers optional)
OPTIONAL:
* Decorative craft hole punches
* "Silly Scissors" (craft scissors that cut variety of decorative lines)

ASSEMBLED SHAPE PUPPETS
1. Cut variety of misc. black cardstock shapes (5 – 8/child)
2. Allow children to explore paper shapes and experiment
on a flat surface, selecting a base shape for their assigned
character, and several small shapes for ears, horns, noses,
hair, etc. Remind them that the face should be a PROFILE
view and that only the outside edge of the shape will show.
Allow 5 – 10 minutes to experiment with shapes before offering glue.
3. Glue shapes together, stapling as needed.
4. Use hole punches to make eyes, etc.
5. Attach bendable straw as rod.

ONE PIECE DRAWN SHAPE PUPPETS

1. Demonstrate that only what is cut, not drawn, shows in the final shape. Allow no more than 5 minutes to draw character on black paper to avoid complex drawings that cannot be cut out.
Remember the pledge!
2. Cut out shape.
3. Use hole punch for eyes, etc.
4. Attach bendable straw or skewer as control rod, depending on age of students.

A simple profile outline like this:

Not this:

JOINTED DRAWN SHAPE PUPPETS

1. Demonstrate that only what is cut, not drawn, shows in the final shape.
2. Demonstrate that any parts intended to move (legs, arms, jaw, tail, etc.) must be CUT AS A SEPARATE PIECE WITH SPACE TO OVERLAP and leave enough paper to punch a hole that is not so close to the edge that it will tear.
TIP: PRINT IN ADVANCE the **SHADOW PUPPET TIPS PAGES** for reference as students draw and cut out their puppets.
3. Allow 15-30 minutes to draw and cut out character parts using sturdy paper.
Remember pledge (especially important when adding moving parts!)
4. Use hole punch for joints, eyes, etc.
5. Attach jointed parts.
6. Attach bamboo skewers. **No puppet (including those with more than one joint) should have more than two rods as we have only two hands to hold them.**

SHADOW PUPPETS ON THE OVERHEAD PROJECTOR

Puppet construction is the same as above, EXCEPT puppets do not need to be made of black paper. (Recycled file folders are perfect.) The rods are attached perpendicular to the puppet, or may need only a paper handle. The puppets are manipulated right on the glass of the overhead projector, and the image is projected onto a screen. Rods must be held at a slight slant to avoid a shadow of the puppeteer's hand. This is a versatile technique, lending itself to much creative experimentation by students grades three and up.

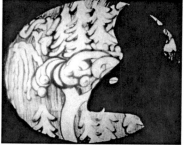

Above, students using projector.
Top right, scene incorporating colored gels.
Bottom, scene incorporating sand drawing, both by author.

SHADOW PUPPET TIPS # 1
MAKING THE PUPPET

Decide which parts you need to move to tell your story:
If the character will be chased, maybe a leg.
If the character talks or eats, maybe the mouth.
Minor characters do not have to have any moving parts.
REMEMBER: ANY moving part is cut as a separate piece.

Make puppets in
PROFILE view

THIS   NOT THIS

CUT

ASSEMBLED

CUT

ASSEMBLED

CUT

ASSEMBLED

CUT

ASSEMBLED

CUT

ASSEMBLED

CUT

ASSEMBLED

SHADOW PUPPET TIPS # 2

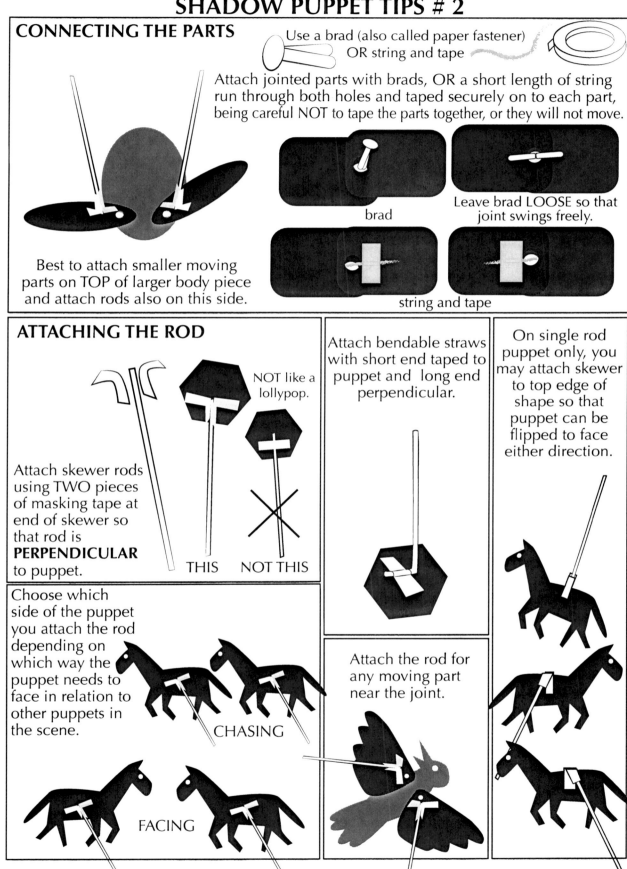

CONNECTING THE PARTS

Use a brad (also called paper fastener) OR string and tape

Attach jointed parts with brads, OR a short length of string run through both holes and taped securely on to each part, being careful NOT to tape the parts together, or they will not move.

brad

Leave brad LOOSE so that joint swings freely.

Best to attach smaller moving parts on TOP of larger body piece and attach rods also on this side.

string and tape

ATTACHING THE ROD

NOT like a lollypop.

Attach skewer rods using TWO pieces of masking tape at end of skewer so that rod is **PERPENDICULAR** to puppet.

THIS   NOT THIS

Choose which side of the puppet you attach the rod depending on which way the puppet needs to face in relation to other puppets in the scene.

CHASING

FACING

Attach bendable straws with short end taped to puppet and long end perpendicular.

Attach the rod for any moving part near the joint.

On single rod puppet only, you may attach skewer to top edge of shape so that puppet can be flipped to face either direction.

TABLE TOP PUPPETS

Table top theater has many variations, featuring puppets that are manipulated on a table top, with the puppeteer(s) standing behind or to the side and sometimes interacting with the puppets.

Bottle chefs, wearing hats made of coffee filters and tape

IN PERFORMANCE

Table top theater can be staged using a plain top of a table. Scenic elements can be placed on the table, and since the puppeteers are fully visible at all times, there is no need to conceal scene changes. The puppets are manipulated with a vertical rod, or simply by the puppeteer's hand directly on the puppet. They may bring history or geography to life moving on a large map on a table top. Box houses, boats, cars, etc. may be built and decorated for the puppets as well. Table top puppets may be used as creative dramatics to bring to life a scene for the participants only, without an audience.

In tabletop performance with an audience, it is very important that the puppeteer consciously avoid eye contact with the audience UNLESS they are intending to interact directly with audience members. However, if they want the audience focus on the puppets, their focus must also at all times be on the puppets.

BOTTLE BUDDIES

• clean 8 or 12 ounce (250ml) plastic bottle
OPTIONAL: to color bottles:
- wrap with masking tape and paint
- prep at least a week in advance as follows: Pour ordinary latex (NOT tempera – it will crack off) paint into each bottle, swirl around, and pour out into the next bottle. Drain the bottles upside down in cardboard boxes. When drained, turn right side up and allow to dry. This gives a shiny, bright color that will not crack off.

• poster board OR (flat) bicycle inner tubes cut as large feet *The flat inner tubes work great as they have some stabilizing weight to them, can be cut with scissors, and are free at bike repair shops.*
• two pipe cleaners per puppet
• fabric scraps, wiggly eyes, yarn, buttons, pom-poms, etc.
• glue gun
• scissors

1.

1. Hot glue feet to stick out from bottle bottom to stabilize puppet.

2. Tightly twist together two pipe cleaners.

3. Attach center with clear packing tape to back to form arms that stick out on each side. Fold and twist pipe cleaner ends to form hands.

4. Decorate character using glue guns to attach wiggly eyes, pompoms, buttons, fabric scraps, yarn wigs, etc.

I would say the only drawback of this project is that all decorations should be attached with hot glue to adhere to plastic, so younger children need to be kept busy choosing and cutting their materials while adults do the gluing.

OPTIONAL: Flat tray-like boxes may be decorated as houses for the puppets, marking rooms and furniture by collage, paint, or markers.

WOOD ROD AND HEAD

- 12" (30cm) thin dowel (sometimes sold as cake supports) or sturdy bamboo skewer or long chop stick or 3/8" or ¼" (6mm) dowels cut in 10 – 12" (25cm) lengths.
- 1" (2.5cm) wood ball, preferably with pre-drilled hole all the way through or two 1-2"(2.5-5cm) poster board circles. Small stirofoam balls are NOT recommended as they split and fall apart and cannot be glued back together.
- 9-10" (25cm) circle of very soft, preferable knit, fabric.
- 12" (30cm) pipe cleaner, cut in half
- small wiggly eyes, permanent markers, yarn
- craft glue, hot glue for quicker drying

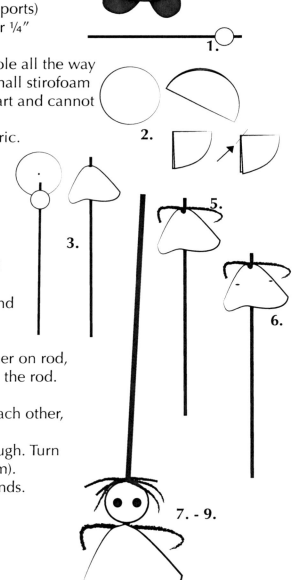

1. Attach ball, or paper circles, to rod, inserting rod into hole, or layering two paper circles and gluing to rod, leaving about ½ " (12mm) of rod protruding.

2. Fold fabric in quarters and snip tiny point from fold corner.

3. Open fabric and insert short end of rod into hole and glue.

4. Cut a pipe cleaner in half and bend in half.

5. Apply craft glue to rod and place fold of pipe cleaner on rod, then make a couple winds of the pipe cleaner around the rod. These will form the arms.

6. Cut two very small snips in fabric circle opposite each other, about 1" (2.5cm) from center.

7. Insert pipe cleaner ends in each hole and pull through. Turn rod right side up (with rod at top and puppet at bottom).

8. Bend over pipe cleaner ends slightly to indicate hands.

9. Decorate face, add yarn wig with craft glue.

TOY THEATRE

In the Victorian era, toy theater traditions featured printed paper sets of opera and theater casts purchased, taken home, and cut out for parlor re-enactments of staged theater. It is now popular for many experimental styles in performances for adults as well as children.

Set and puppet by author for original story.

IN PERFORMANCE
Intended for a small audience, stories of all kinds can be told complete with scene changes. Depending on the size of the box and puppets, puppeteer teams of 1-4 people are best.

THE THEATER
A cardboard box makes a perfect base for toy theatre.
1. Cut a proscenium hole in one side
2. Cut an access slot for the puppets on the top and both sides so that puppets may enter and exit from either side.
3. The box may be decorated.
4. Decorated paper scenes may be raised and lowered in an additional slot made at the back of the stage area.

Scenery painted or collaged on paper or fabric, may be attached to a thin dowel to hang in rear slot.

MINI TOY THEATER
1. Use a shoebox for the stage.
2. Set so that the box opening is on the side.
3. Cut a slot about 1"(2.5cm.) wide the length of the side that is now the top.

162

QUICK CONSTRUCTION PAPER PUPPETS

1. Draw characters onto construction paper.
2. Cut out shape.
3. Decorate both sides of puppet with markers.
3. Attach a bamboo skewer (or sturdy broom straw, popsicle sticks, or plastic drinking straw for younger children) at the top of the head with tape.

Match box size to puppet size and rod length, making sure the rods are long enough that fingers do not show inside stage area.

COLLAGE PUPPETS

1. Cut character shapes out of sturdy paper such as recycled file folders or cereal boxes.
2. Attach a bamboo skewer at the top of the head with tape.
3. Cut magazine photos of faces, clothes, etc. and glue on along with construction paper shapes.
4. Add tiny wiggly eyes, small scraps of fabric and yarn, etc. if desired, making sure puppet does not become too bulky.

Profile (side view) puppets should be decorated on both sides so they may cross stage in either direction. Front view may be decorated only on the front as long as they do not need to turn around on stage.

WOOD ROD AND HEAD puppets on Table Top Theater page may also be used in toy theater.

NOTES ON PROJECT CHECKLIST USE

Following are check lists for each of four puppetry techniques. The purpose of these are to define and clarify each step of the project, including:

- working collaboratively
- story writing
- puppet making
- responsibility for materials and tools
- manipulation tips
- performance criteria for each puppetry technique
- role of the audience

Each group should select one Project Check List Manager who is in charge of checking off items as completed.

In rehearsal, if possible, a member of another group may be selected as Director – to make sure the Performance Elements on the checklist are adhered to.

I have found these checklists to be very useful, since, if every item is checked, all project steps and goals are met.

SUPPLEMENTS & RESOURCES

HAND AND ROD PUPPET PROJECT CHECKLIST AND PERFORMANCE CRITERIA

GROUP MEMBERS: _____

_____

PREPARATION: OUR GROUP (check as each part is completed)
> worked together to complete the STORY PLANNING SHEET by:

____ a. listening to everyone's ideas.

____ b. sharing our own ideas.

____ c. writing down only short sentences - NOT every word the characters speak.

____ built the puppets as instructed.

____ made extra large eyes and noses to be sure the audience could see them.

____ attached hands with thumbs pointing up.

____ finished all puppets required for the story.

____ used the tools properly and put them away when finished.

____ did not waste materials.

____ practiced the story.

____ helped to tell the story we had agreed on.

PERFORMANCE ELEMENTS FOR CRITIQUE

Use the following for rehearsal goals, and for basis of Constructive Critique in rehearsal.

____ The story is written around the assigned topic.

____ The story has a clear beginning, middle, and end.

____ The puppets are held high enough for the audience to see their bodies.

____ The puppets mainly face the audience.

____ Puppets enter and exit either from one side, or as climbing stairs, – not just popping up or down.

____ Puppets make conversations clear by moving when talking, being still when silent.

____ The puppets' movements have purpose: to show action and emotion.

____ The puppets enter and exit the stage at the right times to tell the story.

____ Loud, clear, un-rushed voices – whether narrator, or puppeteers' - allow audience to hear.

____ The group does not bring their STORY PLANNING SHEET to the stage.

____ As performers or audience, group members are polite and respectful at all times.

MIMING PUPPET PROJECT CHECKLIST AND PERFORMANCE CRITERIA

GROUP MEMBERS: _____

_____

PREPARATION: OUR GROUP (check as each part is completed)

        worked together to plan the presentation by:

____   a. doing enough research from several sources to be familiar with the characters (for history based project)

____   b. listening to our partners' ideas.

____   c. sharing our own ideas.

____   d. writing down only short sentences - NOT every word the characters speak.

____   built the puppets as instructed.

____   made sure our puppets had noses that form a strong side view profile shape

____   selected very lightweight puppet clothing material

____   finished all puppets and props required for the story.

____   used the tools properly and put them away when finished.

____   did not waste materials.

____   practiced the presentation.

____   helped to tell the story we had agreed on.

PERFORMANCE ELEMENTS FOR CRITIQUE

Use the following for rehearsal goals, and for basis of Constructive Critique in rehearsal.

____   The presentation is written around the assigned topic.

____   The presentation has a clear beginning, middle, and end.

____   Puppets are held so that the audience sees their bodies, above bottom edge of clothing

____   Puppets face the audience., "cheating out" to face each other at an angle in conversation

____   Puppets make conversations clear by moving when talking, using hand gesture

____   The puppets' movements have purpose: to show action and emotion.

____   If no back curtain, puppeteers DO NOT make eye contact with audience, but remain strongly focused on their puppet.

____   Loud, clear, un-rushed voices allow the audience to hear.

____   The group does not bring script or notes to the stage.

____   As performers or audience, group members are polite and respectful at all times.

SHADOW PUPPET PROJECT CHECKLIST AND PERFORMANCE CRITERIA

GROUP MEMBERS: _____

_____

PREPARATION: OUR GROUP (check as each part is completed)

      worked together to complete the STORY PLANNING SHEET by:

___   a. listening to everyone's ideas.

___   b. sharing our own ideas.

___   c. writing down only short sentences - NOT every word the characters speak.

___   finished all puppets required for the story.

___   made the puppets about the size of our hands.

___   made the puppets' heads shown as profiles (side view).

___   attached the rods so that the puppets face the direction they need to.

___   used the tools properly and put them away when finished.

___   did not waste materials.

___   practiced the story.

___   helped to tell the story we had agreed on.

PERFORMANCE ELEMENTS FOR CRITIQUE

Use the following for rehearsal goals, and for basis of Constructive Critique in rehearsal.

___   The story is written around the assigned topic.

___   The story has a clear beginning, middle, and end.

___   The puppets are held flat against the shadow screen, to make sharp shadows.

___   The puppets enter from one side of the screen and move across the screen as needed.
       They DO NOT suddenly appear or disappear, unless that is intended for the story action.

___   One puppet is introduced at a time when possible - to allow audience to know who they are.

___   The puppets' movements have purpose: to show action and speaking.

___   Puppets make conversations clear by moving when talking, being still when silent.

___   The puppets enter and exit the stage at the right times to tell the story.

___   The group does not bring their STORY PLANNING SHEET to the stage.

___   Loud, clear, un-rushed voices– whether a narrator, or puppeteers' - allow audience to hear.

___   As performers or audience, group members are polite and respectful at all times.

TOY THEATER PROJECT CHECKLIST AND PERFORMANCE CRITERIA

GROUP MEMBERS: _____

_____

PREPARATION: OUR GROUP (check as each part is completed)

worked together to complete the STORY PLANNING SHEET by:

____ a. listening to everyone's ideas.

____ b. sharing our own ideas.

____ c. writing down only short sentences - NOT every word the characters speak.

____ built our stage setting as required for our story

____ built the puppets as instructed.

____ finished all puppets required for the story.

____ used the tools properly and put them away when finished.

____ did not waste materials.

____ practiced the story.

____ helped to tell the story we had agreed on.

PERFORMANCE ELEMENTS FOR CRITIQUE

Use the following for rehearsal goals, and for basis of Constructive Critique in rehearsal.

____ The story is written around the assigned topic.

____ The story has a clear beginning, middle, and end.

____ The puppets enter and exit from the sides of the theater, unless there is reason for top entrance.

____ The puppets flat sides, not edges, face the audience.

____ Puppets make conversations clear by moving when talking, being still when silent.

____ The puppets' movements have purpose: to show action and emotion.

____ The puppets enter and exit the stage at the right times to tell the story.

____ Loud, clear, un-rushed voices– whether a narrator, or puppeteers' - allow audience to hear.

____ The group does not bring their STORY PLANNING SHEET to the stage.

____ As performers or audience, group members are polite and respectful at all times.

TEAMWORK AND FOCUS RUBRIC GRADES 3 – 5

	AT STANDARD	APPROACHING STANDARD	BELOW STANDARD
COLLABORATION	I complete project work on time on my own.	I do some project work but need to be reminded.	My project work is often not done on time.
	I contribute to discussions by listening to team members' ideas as well as contributing my own ideas.	I listen but do not add my ideas, OR I talk without listening to my team members.	I need to learn how to participate in group discussions.
	I am polite and kind to my team members, even if I disagree with them.	I am usually polite and kind, but may stop listening if I disagree with someone.	I am sometimes impolite and unkind, especially if I disagree with someone.
	I help my team members as needed.	I sometimes offer to help my team members.	I need to learn to offer help if someone needs it.
CRITICAL THINKING	I reflected on our assigned topic or theme before adding story ideas.	I thought a little about the theme but got distracted.	I disrupted my team by adding unrelated ideas.
	In Constructive Critiques, I watched the performance and gave polite, helpful comments.	In Constructive Critiques, I watched the show but did not think much about it.	In Constructive Critiques, I did not pay attention to the show, OR I gave disrespectful comments.
COMMUNICATION	I tried to move my puppet as recommended on the Project Checklist.	I looked at the Project Checklist but did not pay much attention to it.	I did not look at the Project Checklist and moved my puppet as I wanted to.
	I cooperated backstage by helping as needed and getting out of the way when my puppet was not on stage.	I stood near the stage even when my puppet was off stage.	I distracted my teammates backstage by teasing or laughing.
CREATIVITY	I shared new ideas of my own in the story writing process as well as in constructing my puppet.	I used story and puppet appearance ideas from movies or TV.	I could not think of any ideas of my own, or I copied what I saw others doing.

CONSTRUCTIVE CRITIQUE PROCESS

It is a rewarding experience for any performer to know what the audience thinks of their work. Peer feedback encourages critical thinking and understanding that, although this process is fun, there are standards to strive for. Students come to look forward to the response allowed through this critique process.

1. After each team's full rehearsal in front of the class, ask the performers to stand in front of the performance area facing their audience.
Make clear that this is an opportunity for them to listen (only) to audience response to their work. They should not feel that they will be required to defend their work.

2. Begin by asking the audience for positive audience comments – what peers thought worked well in the performance. These comments may be based on the elements on the project checklist for the particular technique, such as:
Did performers tell the story agreed on?
Were voices loud enough?
Were puppet movements expressive of action? Emotions?
Could you tell who was speaking?
Were puppets held so the audience could see their movement?
Comments may also address elements such as use of humor, audience interaction, puppet construction, specific comments on effective use of puppet movement, relevance or connection to current events, etc.

3. Following the positive comments, ask audience for polite suggestions for what they could do to improve the work the next time it is performed.
All commnets must be polite and respectful of the performers' work.

TIP: It is a good idea to set a specific number for both positive comments and suggestions for improvement, such as three positive and one or two suggestions for improvement.

Sound Effects Orchestra

A highly effective addition to many of these projects, when telling a story involving the whole class, is the sound effects orchestra.
It requires a collection of percussion sound effects of all kinds: coconut shell cut in half, recycled bottle shakers containing beans, rice, or sand, for different sounds, chimes, bells, scrapers, maracas, castanets, rain sticks, small drums, and, of course, NOT including any sound effects that require blowing with the mouth.

I have a trunk full of these, collected while traveling, from thrift stores, some purchased at music or toy stores.

For story based project:
Divide the class and construct puppets so that there is a double cast of characters.

For more free form project, such as poetry, simply divide class in half and take turns being puppeteer or sound effects orchestra member.

While one group is performing with their puppets, the other is providing appropriate sound effects for the entrance and movement of their assigned character or dramatic event. *It is important to assign sounds in advance, so everyone knows which sound goes with which character or event in the story.*

I often assign teams of two, who each build puppets of the same character, and each provide the sound effect for the other during performance.

Sound assignments can be totally creative and selected by the students – footsteps sounds of different characters, crossing a river sound, wind, a butterfly sound, and danger sound, a surprise sound, a thinking out a problem sound, etc.

I have found the sound effects orchestra to be highly effective for self-discipline. Students understand quickly the consequences if they lose their sound effect when it is used inappropriately. The process also facilitates focus and teamwork, as when someone forgets to make their sound when needed, other students usually remind them. I find many students who prefer making the sound effects to operating a puppet, so sharing roles gives opportunity for both experiences.

REFERENCES

PUPPETRY BOOKS
Worlds of Shadow: Teaching with Shadow Puppetry, by David Wisniewski and Donna Wisniewski
Practical, well written lessons, including lots of creative ideas for the overhead projector. If your school has thrown these out as outdated technology, available cheap used at online sources. Highly recommended!

The Complete Book of Puppetry, by George Latshaw
A practical, classic and timeless work for puppeteers at any level.

Theatre on a Tabletop: Puppetry for Small Spaces, by Kuang-Yu Fong and Stephen Kaplin
A practical as well as philosophical guide.

IMAGINATION: At Play with Puppets and Creative Drama, by Nancy Frazier and Nancy Renfro
Highly creative arts integrated lessons using very simple materials.

Puppet Shows Made Easy, by Nancy Renfro
Any book by the late Nancy Renfro is timeless and practical.

Puppets and Masks: Stagecraft and Storytelling, by Nan Rump
Lots of creative, story-related construction ideas using simple materials.

A Show of Hands: Using Puppets with Young Chidren, by Ingrid M. Crepeau & M. Ann Richards
Specific lessons and creative construction ideas.

Puppetry in Early Childhood Education, by Tamara Hunt and Nancy Renfro
Many practical and specific lessons and ideas for the very young child.

The Puppetry Handbook, by Anita Sinclair
Excellent, practical book for puppeteers at all levels.

EDUCATION BOOKS
Comprehension Connections: Bridges to Strategic Reading, by Tanny McGregor

Talking, Drawing, Writing: Lessons for Our Youngest Writers, by Martha Horn and Mary Ellen Giacobbe

PBL in the Elementary Grades: Step-by-Step Guidance, Tools, and Tips for Standards-Focused K-5 Projects, from the Buck Institute for Education

Visual Thinking Strategies, by Philip Yenawine

ONLINE
Puppeteers of America: www.puppeteers.org
Union Internationale de la Marionette: www.unima.org

CPSIA information can be obtained
at www.ICGtesting.com
Printed in the USA
LVOW09s1820070617
537271LV00007B/358/P